Holiday Recipes

150 Easy Recipes and Gifts from Your Kitchen

Bonnie Scott

Graphics by Cheryl Seslar Designs

ISBN-13: 978-1480179158

TABLE OF CONTENTS

Holiday Recipes

Give a gift of love this holiday season with homemade favorites from your kitchen. Everyone leads such busy lives, and gifts from your kitchen are thoughtful and much appreciated tokens of affection for family, friends and co-workers.

Maybe you're the Cookie Queen, Baroness of Bars or the Candy Countess. Whatever style cooking is your passion, you're sure to find something new and exciting in this extensive collection of home crafted recipes. There are snacks, savories, drinks, hors d'oeuvres and desserts of all kinds to tempt your family's taste buds and add pizzazz to any host's buffet table.

This collection includes strategies to make your preparations easier, as well as tips to make your finished products tastier and more attractive. We also include loads of unique ideas to package your creations for gifts that are memorable and maybe even photo worthy. Combine your handcrafted culinary creations with a thoughtful kitchen accessory or decorative item to create a one-of-a-kind gift that will be enjoyed now and appreciated for years to come.

When you're giving gifts of food, make it extra special by including the original recipe. Hand write the recipe on colorful recipe cards or print the recipe in an attractive font on a specialty paper or card stock. Make sure you Include any hints or tips you use to create your culinary confections. Don't forget to include your name so the recipient will always remember who gave them that delicious recipe.

Keep reading to find all kinds of ideas for gifts from your kitchen, including an internet address for free printables – Christmas cookie pouches, bag toppers and hang tags for your baked goods.

Bread

Quick breads are fast and delicious. They're a real treat for everyone and a welcome change from the usual holiday cookie and candy routine. Dessert breads aren't usually as sugar-laden as cookies or cake. This makes them a perfect gift for those whose sweet tooth isn't as extreme, since quick breads satisfy that craving for a little bit of dessert.

Baking Tips

Most quick breads store well, so plan a day to get a head start on your holiday baking. Properly wrapped, quick breads can be refrigerated for one week or frozen for two to three months.

If you've got a favorite bread recipe, you can easily adapt it for mini loaves. You don't need to change the ingredients, but you must reduce the baking time. Set your oven to the temperature your recipe recommends. Fill your mini loaf pans one-half to two-thirds full and bake for one-half the recommended time. Check for doneness, and if the center is still too moist, bake in five-minute increments until done.

Wrap Your Mini Loaves with Maximum Style

Make your breads special by baking them in mini loaves and presenting them in festive, holiday wrappings. Added to a gift basket or an assortment of treats, they make any gift extra special.

Once you've completed your baking, it's time to dress up your mini loaves. After wrapping your tasty treats in plastic film, it's time to get creative. There are lots of fun, festive wrappers to download and print out. Cut the paper into strips, wrap the loaf and secure with tape on the bottom. Then you can add a premade bow, ribbon tie or even a tie made of twine or raffia for a country look. Use gift tags with a hole punched at the top to hang from your ribbon, and your mini loaf is ready.

Craft stores have bakery-style gift boxes in many sizes. Place your loaf in a box, wrap a strip of festive paper around it and tie with white string. Use premade paper, or let the kids in on the fun and have them create artwork for your gift boxes.

Brown paper, from either a roll of butcher paper or paper bags, makes an eco-friendly and sophisticated wrapper when tied up with an elegant, wide ribbon. Add a special gift tag to hang from the ribbon and your gift is ready.

For a gift they'll remember long after the last crumb is gone, place your bread on a handsome cutting board and tie with a colorful ribbon. You can wrap the bread in holiday paper or even wrap it in a cloth napkin or useful kitchen towel.

If you've made a variety of breads, cut into generous slices, wrap individually in parchment paper and secure with a tag that indicates the variety. Fill a bakery-style box with a selection of slices, and tie it up with a jaunty ribbon for a 'fresh from the bakery' look.

Here's a trick so you aren't gifting a dirty pan after baking in it. Purchase colorful ceramic mini loaf baking pans and prepare your loaves in these pans. Line the ceramic pan with parchment paper before baking and spray the paper with Pam®. When the loaf is finished baking, you can lift the loaf out of the pan by the parchment paper and wash the pan. Clean the pans to sparkling perfection, wrap the loaves in plastic wrap and replace in the pans. Use a coordinated kitchen towel to wrap your gift and tie the package up with raffia or a silk ribbon.

Banana Nut Bread

1 cup sugar
1 egg
3 ripe bananas
1/2 cup margarine
1 teaspoon vanilla
2 cups flour
1 teaspoon baking soda
1/2 cup nuts, chopped
Optional - 1/2 cup dates, chopped
Optional - 1/2 cup maraschino cherries

In a large bowl, beat egg, margarine, sugar, bananas and vanilla until smooth. Mix flour and baking soda together and blend into banana mixture. Stir in remaining ingredients. Grease 2 5x9 inch loaf pans. Bake at 350 degrees F for 1 hour or until done.

Yield: 2 loaves

Minis: This recipe will make 4 mini-loaves (fill pans 3/4 full with batter) baked for 40 to 45 minutes or until toothpick inserted comes out clean.

Banana Nut Bread Mini Loaves

To achieve this look, purchase some inexpensive ceramic mini bread pans. (These pans are from Bed, Bath and Beyond.) Use cute ribbon about 2 1/2 inches wide. Just wrap the ribbon around the ceramic pans and secure underneath with double stick tape. Add little bows and pompoms to the ribbon for a 3-dimensional look.

Quick Fruity Bread

1 cup sugar
1/2 cup butter
2 1/8 cups flour
1/2 teaspoon salt
2 teaspoons baking powder
2 eggs
1 teaspoon vanilla
1 cup milk
1/2 teaspoon almond extract
3/4 cup raisins
3/4 cup candied fruit
1/2 cup maraschino cherries
1/2 cup dates, chopped
1/2 cup almonds, chopped

Cream sugar and butter together. Add eggs and beat until smooth. Mix in vanilla, milk and almond extract. In a separate bowl, mix flour, salt and baking powder. Mix in raisins, fruit and almonds. Mix the contents of the two bowls together. Bake in a greased 9 x 5" loaf pan at 350 degrees F for one hour or until passes toothpick test.

Yield: 1 loaf

Easy Bread Wrapping

For this effect, first wrap the bread loaf in plastic wrap. Secure with tape or use a layer of shrink wrap over the plastic wrap. Wrap a length of burlap mesh around the bread. Secure it with a couple of stitches or use tape temporarily. Add a length of ribbon and tie a bow.

Eggnog Cherry Bread

3/4 cup sugar
2 1/2 cups flour
1 teaspoon salt
1 tablespoon baking powder
1 egg, beaten
1/3 cup vegetable oil
1 1/4 cup eggnog
1/2 cup chopped walnuts
3/4 cup maraschino cherries, chopped

Mix together sugar, flour, salt and baking powder. In a separate bowl, mix egg, oil and eggnog. Mix egg mixture into dry ingredients. Gently stir in cherries and nuts. Divide mixture between 2 greased 8x4 inch loaf pans. Add a few nuts on top, if desired. Bake at 350 degrees F for 40 to 45 minutes.

Yield: 2 loaves

Eggnog Cherry Nut Loaf

These plain paper sacks with handles are available at most craft stores. They are a blank canvas just waiting for your creativity. This is a mini-loaf of bread which fits in the small sack perfectly.

Holiday Chocolate Pumpkin Bread

1 3/4 cups flour
1 teaspoon cinnamon
1 teaspoon pumpkin pie spice
1/2 teaspoon nutmeg
1/2 teaspoon salt
1 teaspoon baking soda
1/2 cup butter
1 cup sugar
2 eggs
1 1/2 cups canned pumpkin
3/4 cup chocolate chips
3/4 cup walnuts

Combine flour, cinnamon, pumpkin pie spice, nutmeg, baking soda and salt. Cream butter and sugar together. Blend in eggs and beat. Add dry ingredients alternately with pumpkin to the butter and sugar mixture. Mix in the chocolate chips and just 1/2 cup of the nuts. Grease the bottom of 9x5 inch loaf pan and pour batter in pan. Sprinkle 1/4 cup nuts on top. Bake at 350 degrees F for 65 to 70 minutes. Cool then drizzle with glaze.

Glaze:

1/2 cup powdered sugar
1/8 teaspoon cinnamon
1/8 teaspoon nutmeg
1 to 2 tablespoons cream

Mix all glaze ingredients together, then microwave for about

20 seconds. Mix well, then drizzle on bread.

Yield: 1 loaf

Minis: This recipe will make 4 mini-loaves (fill pans 3/4 full with batter) baked for 40 to 45 minutes or until they pass the toothpick test.

Cinnamon Twists

1/2 cup sugar
2 teaspoons cinnamon
1 package refrigerated biscuits
1/4 cup margarine, melted
2 tablespoons walnuts, chopped

Combine sugar and cinnamon in a bowl. Let biscuits sit out for 10 to 15 minutes until they are easy to work with. Roll each biscuit into a 9" long rope. Using the 2 ends of the rope, pinch them together to form a circle.

Dip each rope into margarine, then in the sugar cinnamon mix. Twist in shape of an 8. Place on greased baking sheet. Sprinkle with nuts. Bake at 450 degrees F for 10 minutes.

Cherry Pecan Bread

2 cups flour
3/4 cup sugar
1/2 teaspoon salt
1 teaspoon baking soda
1/2 cup vegetable oil
2 eggs, beaten
1 teaspoon vanilla
1 cup buttermilk
1 cup chopped nuts
1/2 cup red maraschino cherries, drained and cut in quarters

In a mixing bowl, stir together sugar, flour, salt and baking soda; set aside. Using another bowl, combine eggs, oil, vanilla and buttermilk. Add to dry ingredients, stirring just until mixed. Fold in nuts and cherries. Pour into a greased 9x5 inch loaf pan. Bake at 350 degrees F for 50 to 55 minutes or until the bread tests done with toothpick.

Smells Like Christmas Pumpkin Bread

3 1/2 cups flour
1 1/2 teaspoon salt
2 teaspoons baking soda
3 cups sugar
1 teaspoon baking powder
2/3 cup water
1 cup oil
5 eggs, beaten
2 teaspoons nutmeg
1 teaspoon allspice
2 teaspoons cinnamon
1/2 teaspoon ground cloves
1 can pumpkin puree, 16 ounces
1 cup pecans, chopped

Preheat oven to 350 degrees F. Grease two 5 x 9 inch loaf pans. Mix together all dry ingredients in a large bowl. Stir in water and oil. Beat eggs and mix into batter. Blend in the pumpkin, then add pecans. Divide batter equally and pour into the 2 pans. Bake for 1 hour or until passes toothpick test. Cool 5 minutes in pan before removing.

Yield: 2 loaves

Very Cherry Bread

2 eggs, beaten well
1 1/2 cups flour
1 cup sugar
1 1/2 teaspoons baking powder
1 5 ounce jar maraschino cherries cut up – juice and all
1/2 cup nuts

Mix together the flour, sugar and baking powder. Mix in the eggs. Add the cherries, cherry juice and nuts.

Bake in a well-greased 9 x 5 inch pan at 350 degrees F for 1 hour.

Yield: 1 loaf

Clear plastic Cello bags or treat bags with a design as in the picture above are available at craft stores. A mini loaf of bread fits perfectly in the large bags. Visit www.NorthPoleChristmas.com/holiday.html to print the 7" bag toppers and crop them to whatever size is needed.

Date Nut Bread

1 cup dates, chopped
2 cups boiling water
2 teaspoons baking soda
1 1/2 cups brown sugar
2 eggs
2 cups flour
1 tablespoon butter
1/4 teaspoon salt

Mix together dates, water and baking soda. Let cool. Mix brown sugar, eggs, flour, butter and salt together. Mix in date mixture and pour in a loaf pan. Bake 45 minutes at 350 degrees.

Yield: 1 loaf

Monkey Bread

4 cans Pillsbury® buttermilk biscuits
1/2 cup white sugar
3 teaspoons cinnamon
2 cups pecans, chopped
1 cup brown sugar
1/2 cup butter
1 teaspoon Karo® corn syrup

Preheat oven to 350 degrees F. Grease a Bundt pan. Cut biscuits into fourths. Mix the sugar and cinnamon together in a bowl. Roll dough pieces in sugar and cinnamon. Lay the biscuits and nuts in the pan in layers.

Put butter and brown sugar in a saucepan and bring to a boil for one minute. Add Karo® syrup to butter and brown sugar. Pour over biscuits and bake for 35 minutes. Invert on serving plate. Let stand for 5 minutes, allowing caramel to drizzle down. Remove from pan.

Festive Pumpkin Bread

3 1/2 cups flour
1 teaspoon pumpkin pie spice
1 teaspoon ground cinnamon
1 teaspoon baking powder
1 teaspoon ground nutmeg
2 teaspoons baking soda
2 1/2 cups solid pack pumpkin
1 cup vegetable oil
2 1/2 cups sugar
3 eggs
1 cup raisins
1 cup walnuts, chopped

Preheat oven to 350 degrees F. In a bowl, mix the flour, baking powder, pumpkin pie spice, baking soda, cinnamon and nutmeg together. Set aside. In a bowl, mix the pumpkin, oil, sugar and eggs. Beat with mixer until well blended. Add dry ingredients and mix well. By hand, stir in the raisins and walnuts. Spray 2 loaf pans with non-stick cooking spray. Pour the batter in the 2 pans. Bake for 50 to 55 minutes. Cool before glazing.

Sweet Glaze:

1 1/2 cup confectioner's sugar
1 teaspoon grated orange peel
6 teaspoon orange juice
Walnuts, chopped

Mix confectioner's sugar, orange peel and juice in a bowl. Use spoon to pour glaze over the loaves, letting it run down the sides. Sprinkle walnuts on the loaf before glaze hardens.

Panettone Italian Bread

2 eggs
1 teaspoon vanilla extract
1/4 teaspoon salt
1/4 cup sugar
1 pkg. active dry yeast, .25 oz.
1 cup warm water (110 degrees F)
1/2 cup plain yogurt, nonfat
4 cups all-purpose flour
1/4 cup dried currants
1/2 cup sweet raisins
1 tablespoon lemon zest, grated
1 tablespoon butter, melted
1 tablespoon confectioners' sugar

Mix together water, sugar and yeast in a medium sized mixing bowl. Once mixed, cover bowl and let stand for approximately 10 minutes, or until mixture is foamy. Add to mixture the following: lemon zest, vanilla, eggs, salt and yogurt and mix well. Mix in the flour a little at a time until the dough forms a ball that is manageable.

On a lightly floured surface, knead dough for 5 to 10 minutes, add more flour if needed. Dough should be soft and workable, not sticky. Lightly spray a mixing bowl with non-stick spray, place dough in the bowl, cover and let the dough rise in a warm area until it has doubled, approximately 60 minutes.

Spray an 8 inch round cake pan with non-stick cooking spray. Place confectioners' sugar and dried fruit in a bowl and mix. Punch down the dough in the bowl, then place on floured surface and knead the fruit into the dough.

Form the dough into a ball and place it into the 8" cake pan. Cover cake pan with tea towel, let the dough rise for 30 minutes. (Dough will rise above the cake pan.) Brush melted butter on top of dough. Bake for 45 minutes at 350 degrees F, until loaf is golden brown. Inserted toothpick should come out clean.

Dipper Ginger Shortbread

1/2 cup butter, softened
1/3 cup brown sugar, packed
1 cup flour
1/2 teaspoon ground ginger
1 cup semisweet chocolate chips, melted

Preheat oven to 300 degrees F. In a large bowl, cream butter and sugar until fluffy. In a medium bowl, mix together flour and ginger. Stir dry ingredients into creamed mixture; knead until a soft dough forms.

Press dough into bottom of a greased 8-inch round shortbread mold or a 9-inch round cake pan. Prick shortbread with a fork. Bake 30 to 35 minutes or until light brown. Cool in pan 10 minutes. Cut into wedges on a cutting board while shortbread is warm. Cool completely.

Dip wide end of each piece of shortbread in melted chocolate. Transfer to a wire rack with waxed paper underneath to cool completely.

Breadstick Pretzels

Breadstick dough
1 egg, beaten
Salt

Form pretzel shapes with breadstick dough. Place on a greased cookie sheet. Brush each pretzel with egg and sprinkle with salt. Bake in the oven for 10 minutes at 425 degrees F until golden brown.

Pistachio Bread

1 package yellow cake mix, 18 ounces
2 packages instant pistachio pudding mix, 3 ounces each
2 tablespoons water
1/2 cup maraschino cherries
1/2 teaspoon ground cinnamon
2 tablespoons white sugar
1 cup sour cream
4 eggs
1/4 cup vegetable oil

Mix together cake mix, oil, water, eggs, pudding mix, sour cream and cherries. Pour into 2 greased and floured 9x5" loaf pans. In a bowl, mix the sugar and cinnamon together and sprinkle it on top of the loaves. Bake for 45 minutes at 350 degrees F.

Yield: 2 loaves

Takeout Gift Containers

Most craft stores carry decorative takeout containers. They are the perfect size for gifting a full size loaf of bread. Add some cocoa drink packets and relaxing is in someone's future.

Sticky Rolls

1 package frozen white dinner rolls
1 package dry butterscotch pudding
1/2 cup brown sugar
1/2 cup chopped nuts
1 teaspoon cinnamon
1/2 cup melted butter

In angel food pan, place rolls on top of each other. Mix together the cinnamon, brown sugar, pudding mix and nuts and sprinkle on top of the rolls. Drizzle melted butter over brown sugar mixture. Place waxed paper over top. Leave the rolls out overnight to rise. In the morning, bake at 350 degrees F for 25 minutes. Invert onto serving platter.

Yield: 6 to 8 servings

Mini Pistachio Loaves

Instant pistachio pudding mix, 3 1/2 ounces
1 package yellow cake mix, 18 ounces
4 eggs
1 cup sour cream
11/4 cup water
1/4 cup vegetable oil
2 1/2 teaspoons cinnamon
3/4 cup pecans, chopped
3 tablespoons brown sugar
1/2 cup red maraschino cherries

In a mixing bowl, combine cake and pudding mixes. Add eggs, sour cream, water and oil and beat until well mixed. Pour into five greased 6 x 3 x 2" small loaf pans. Combine the cinnamon, pecans, cherries and brown sugar and spread over batter. Bake at 350° for 35 to 40 minutes or until passes the toothpick test.

Yield: 5 mini-loaves

Easy Banana Bread

1/2 cup margarine
1 cup sugar
1 teaspoon vanilla
3 or 4 ripe bananas
2 eggs
2 cups flour
1 teaspoon baking soda
1/2 teaspoon salt

Preheat oven to 350 degrees F. Cream sugar and margarine in a large mixing bowl. Add eggs one at a time, beating after each one until light and fluffy. Blend in vanilla. Mash bananas and add to creamed mixture alternatively with the flour. Mix only until ingredients are blended together. Do not overbeat. Mix in the baking soda and salt. Place mixture in large greased loaf pan. Bake for 55 to 60 minutes.

Yield: 1 loaf

Mini-Baskets

Baskets are excellent for gifting mini-loaves of bread. Just add a couple squares of fabric to cushion the gift from your kitchen and it's all wrapped.

Candy and Nuts

Your friends and relatives have probably come to expect a sweet treat from you during the holidays. Candy and nut confections just shout 'Holiday.' Most of us reserve these special recipes for the season and pull out all the stops for creating specialties to treat everyone on our gift-giving list. With all the fun and creative recipes we've assembled, you'll certainly find a few new recipes that will become instant hits with your family.

Candy Making Tips

Use a serrated knife to chop your chocolate before melting. Start with one side and use the sharpness of the serrated edge to easily chunk of bits of chocolate. Rotate the block as you work.

Use your microwave to easily melt chocolate. Chocolate can become grainy or lumpy if overheated, so it must be heated slowly. Use the 50 percent power setting on your microwave oven and heat in 30 second increments. If your microwave does not have the reduced power setting, heat the chocolate in 15 second increments. If your microwave does not have a turntable, rotate the bowl each time you stir the chocolate.

If your recipe calls for butter, never substitute margarine. This product contains water and can change the cooking time and results of your recipe.

Wrap Your Candy And Nuts With Style

There's many ways to wrap your tasty gift. Check your craft store for white bakery-style boxes. You'll find a wide assortment of shapes and sizes. Line a box with colorful tissue paper and fill with your confections. If there's any concern about sticking, place a layer of parchment paper between the layers. Complete your gift with a wide, festive ribbon and bow, and add a colorful gift tag.

Cellophane bags are available in lots of colors and sizes. Fill a bag and tie the top with ribbon. Use curling ribbon to make a cascade of curls that complement the color of the cellophane.

Cover a lidded gift box with wallpaper for a unique, reusable container that becomes part of the gift. Tie up your box with ribbon or thin satin rope. A covered decorator container of wicker, glass, pottery or a metal tin are all thoughtful gift box ideas.

Bag toppers work well with a brown bag. It's a very economical way to go when you want to gift a whole sack of treats. Use the 7" toppers available at www.NorthPoleChristmas.com/holiday.html and cut them to the size required.

Quick Fudge

2/3 cup Carnation® evaporated milk
2 tablespoons butter
1 2/3 cups sugar
1/2 cup walnuts, chopped
1 1/2 cup semi-sweet chocolate chips
2 cups miniature marshmallows
1 teaspoon vanilla

Heat the milk, butter and sugar in a saucepan to boiling. Cook 5 minutes, stirring constantly. Remove from heat. Add walnuts, chocolate chips, marshmallows and vanilla. Stir until marshmallows are melted. Pour into buttered 8 or 9" square pan. Garnish with chopped nuts, if desired.

Tiger Butter Candy

1 package almond bark
1/2 cup crunchy peanut butter
1 1/2 cups semi-sweet chocolate chips

Line a cookie sheet with tin foil. In a pan, melt almond bark and peanut butter together over low heat. While that is melting, melt the chocolate chips in the microwave at 50% power, stirring every 30 seconds.

When melted, pour the almond bark mixture on the foil lined cookie sheet. Drizzle the melted chocolate chips over the almond bark mixture and make swirly designs with a spoon. Refrigerate and break into pieces.

Chocolate Truffles With Almond Chocolate Creme Centers

1 cup whipping cream (liquid)
Semi-sweet chocolate, 10 ounces
3 tablespoons butter
1 1/4 cups coarsely chopped (small) toasted unblanched almonds

Heat whipping cream to simmering. (Medium to medium high heat or will burn... heat until just starts to boil). Remove from heat. Add chocolate and butter. Wisk until smooth. Cool to lukewarm. Then stir in almonds. Refrigerate covered, stirring occasionally for 4 hours or overnight.

Then take spoon and scrape across top to roll into balls. Freeze on baking sheet until hard. Melt chocolate chips or large Hershey bars over hot water (not boiling). Dip candy in using spoon or toothpicks. Put on wax paper on baking sheet. Put in freezer or refrigerator until hard.

(Note: Leave the candy in the freezer and remove just a few at a time for dipping in the chocolate. They will start to unfreeze really fast.)

Yield: 4 1/2 dozen

Spiced Pecans

1 egg white
2 teaspoons water
3 tablespoons sugar
3/4 teaspoon cinnamon
1/8 teaspoon nutmeg
1/8 teaspoon ginger
1 pound pecan halves

Blend egg white and water with fork. Stir in sugar and spices; beat until frothy. Mix with pecans to coat well. Bake 15 minutes at 350 degrees F in a 13 x 9 pan. Cool 5 minutes, then remove from pan.

Coconut Swirls

2 tablespoons butter
3 tablespoons water
1 teaspoon vanilla
1/2 cup Pet® instant dry milk
2 cups powdered sugar
3 cups coconut
Semi-sweet chocolate chips, 12 oz. package

Melt butter in a saucepan. Take from heat and add water and vanilla. In a bowl, mix powdered sugar and instant milk together. Add to butter mixture, about 1/2 cup at a time, mixing well after each addition. Stir in coconut.

Drop spoonfuls of mixture onto waxed paper. Let stand till firm about 10 minutes. Melt chocolate chips over hot (not boiling) water or in microwave. Swirl a teaspoon of melted chocolate on top of each candy, then refrigerate.

Yield: 36 candies

Microwave Fudge

Semi-sweet chocolate chips, 18 oz. package
1 can Eagle Brand® milk
1 teaspoon vanilla
1 1/2 cups pecans

Mix all ingredients together and microwave 1 minute on high. Stir, microwave 1 1/2 minutes more. Add vanilla and pecans. Pour in an 8x8" buttered dish and refrigerate.

Microwave Peanut Brittle

1 cup sugar
1/2 cup raw peanuts
Salt
1/2 cup corn syrup
1 teaspoon butter
1 teaspoon vanilla
1 teaspoon soda

Mix sugar, syrup, salt and peanuts. Cook on high for 4 minutes. Stir. Then cook 5 minutes more. Add vanilla and butter. Cook 2 minutes. Add baking soda and spread on a buttered or greased cookie sheet at once.

Peanut Clusters

1 pound almond bark (white)
1-12 ounce package semi-sweet chocolate chips
1-12 ounce jar dry roasted peanuts

Melt almond bark in double broiler or microwave at 50% power. Add chocolate chips and stir until melted. Add peanuts. Cool and beat until a little firm and drop by spoonfuls onto waxed paper. Cool and store in tins.

Cinnamon Pecans

3/4 to 1 1/4 pounds pecan halves
1 to 2 egg whites, beaten
3/4 to 1 1/4 cup cinnamon sugar

In a large bowl, coat pecan halves with egg whites. Stir in cinnamon sugar, 1/4 cup at a time until no more is absorbed. Spread on cookie sheet. Bake 1 1/2 hours at 175 degrees. Stir every 15 minutes to prevent sticking to pan.

Bourbon Balls

2 boxes powdered sugar
1/2 cup butter, melted
1/3 cup bourbon
8 whole pieces of semi-sweet chocolate bar
3 tablespoons paraffin

Mix 1 box of sugar with the butter. Mix 1 box of sugar with bourbon. Mix together; refrigerate 1 to 2 hours. Roll in balls and put on wax paper on cookie sheet. Melt chocolate and paraffin together. Stick ball on toothpick and drip chocolate mix on top; do not dip. Set on wax paper to dry. Keep refrigerated.

Christmas Date Nut Balls

Pitted dates, 8-oz package, chopped
1 cup sugar
1 egg, beaten
1/2 cup margarine
2 1/2 cups Rice Krispies®
1/2 cup pecans, chopped
1 teaspoon vanilla
2 cans shredded coconut

Put the dates, sugar, egg and margarine in a saucepan over moderate heat and bring the mixture to a boil. Let it boil five minutes, stirring constantly so that the mixture does not stick to the pan. Remove the pan from the heat and let it cool for five minutes. Then add Rice Krispies®, pecans and vanilla and mix lightly.

Form the mixture into 1 inch balls and roll them in shredded coconut.

Yield: 5 dozen

Chewy Noels

1/3 cup flour
1/8 teaspoon baking soda
1/8 teaspoon salt
1 cup nuts, chopped
1 cup brown sugar, packed
1 teaspoon vanilla
2 eggs, beaten
2 tablespoons butter
Confectioner's sugar

Mix together baking soda, flour and salt, then stir in nuts and brown sugar. Add vanilla and eggs. Melt butter and put butter in a 9x9x2" pan. Carefully pour batter on butter in pan. Do not stir. Bake in oven at 350 degrees F for 20 to 25 minutes. Sprinkle with confectioner's sugar. Place waxed paper on wire rack. Invert pan onto rack and cool. Dust cookie bars with confectioner's sugar.

Yield: 24 bars

Hangtags for Baked Goods

All of the hang tags shown above can be printed at www.NorthPoleChristmas.com/holiday.html

English Toffee Treats

1 cup butter
1 1/2 cups brown sugar, packed
2 cups whole walnuts
Chocolate chips, 12 ounces

Mix the butter and brown sugar in a saucepan. Boil for 7 minutes. Lay out the walnuts on a greased baking sheet. Pour the butter mixture over the nuts. Sprinkle the chocolate chips on top. Let set until soft and spread chocolate over candy. Cool, break into pieces.

Ting-A-Lings

14 ounces semi-sweet chocolate chips
4 cups corn flakes

Melt chocolate chips; cool to room temperature. Gently stir in corn flakes until well coated. Drop by spoonfuls onto waxed paper or foil. Refrigerate until set, about 2 hours.

No-Bake Holiday Balls

1/2 cup butter, softened
1 tablespoon milk
1 1/2 cups confectioners' sugar
1 teaspoon vanilla extract
1 1/2 cups shredded coconut
2 - 6 ounce jars maraschino cherries
Graham cracker crumbs, finely crushed

In a bowl, mix butter, milk, sugar and vanilla together until smooth. Add coconut and mix well. Refrigerate for 1 hour. In the meantime, let the cherries drain on paper towels. When chilled, shape a tablespoonful of the coconut mix around each cherry. Roll the ball in graham cracker crumbs. Freeze or refrigerate until serving.

Yield: 2 1/2 dozen

Chocolate Fudge

2 8 ounce cans Eagle Brand® milk
2 12 ounce bags chocolate chips
1 12 ounce bag butterscotch chips
1 12 ounce jar marshmallow cream
2 teaspoons vanilla flavoring
1 teaspoon salt
2 cups chopped nuts

Melt chocolate chips and butterscotch chips with milk. Bring to boil. Add marshmallow cream, vanilla flavoring and salt. Mix well. Add nuts. Mix well and pour into dish to cool. Cut into squares.

Yield: 36 2” squares.

Peppermint Brittle

30 small peppermint candy canes or 4 regular candy canes
2 pounds white chocolate

Melt the white chocolate in the microwave, stirring occasionally. Break the candy canes into small pieces. (Putting the candy canes in a couple of Ziploc bags and smashing them with a rolling pin or hammer works well.)

Add most of the candy cane pieces to the melted chocolate and stir to mix. Spread mixture thinly on a wax paper or parchment paper lined cookie sheet.

Sprinkle the remaining candy cane pieces on top, along with the "peppermint dust". Refrigerate until hard, about 30 minutes. Break into pieces.

Peppermint Brittle

Sugar Coated Pecans

2 egg whites
1 tablespoon water
1 teaspoon of vanilla
1 pound pecan halves
3/4 teaspoon salt
1 cup white sugar
1 teaspoon ground cinnamon

In a medium bowl, whip the egg whites and water together until foamy. Add vanilla. In a separate bowl, mix the salt, sugar and cinnamon together.

Add the pecans to the egg white mix and stir to coat the pecans. Lift the pecans out of the egg white mix with a slotted spoon and mix them in the sugar mixture until well covered. (Or put the sugar mixture in a large Ziploc® bag, then add the nuts to coat.) Lay the nuts out on a parchment paper covered or greased cookie sheet. Bake at 250 degrees F for 1 hour, stirring every 15 minutes.

Chocolate Balls

1 can Eagle Brand® sweetened condensed milk
1 package 6 ounce chocolate chips
1 cup coconut shredded
1/2 teaspoon baking soda
Confectioners' sugar

Mix all ingredients together. Line 8 x 8 inch pan with foil. Grease foil very well. Place mixture in pan. Bake at 350 degrees F for 1/2 hour or until brown on top. Cool. Take a teaspoonful, drop in powdered sugar and roll into a ball. Let set. Can be frozen.

Yield: 32 balls

Cheese Balls

There are cheese balls for every taste. Savory herbal combinations, sweet and fruity tastes or tangy cheese filled flavors are sure to be a hit this holiday season. A cheese ball makes a welcome hostess gift when attending a party or is great for a busy family. Kids, as well as adults, will enjoy this no fuss treat.

Preparation Tips For Cheese Balls And Logs

Make sure to use the freshest of ingredients when preparing your cheese balls. Ingredients should be finely minced or crushed.

All ingredients should be at room temperature to make mixing quick and easy. After blending all the ingredients, scrape the mixture into a plastic film or parchment lined bowl and chill. Chill the mixture before shaping into balls.

If your cheese ball will be covered with nuts, toast the nuts in the oven for extra flavor. Cool to room temperature before coating the ball.

Cheese balls should not be frozen. Frozen cheese losses some of its flavor and the ingredients may separate upon thawing, so prepare these savory selections within a day or two of gift giving time.

Use nuts, seeds or herbs as a coating for savory cheese balls. Sweet cheese balls can be covered with nuts or shredded coconut.

Festive Wraps Make Cheese Balls A Welcome Gift

Cheese balls should be refrigerated until it's time for gift giving. Wrap the ball securely in plastic film and keep refrigerated until you're ready for the final presentation.

Craft stores have Shaker style wooden boxes with lids that are inexpensive and ready to decorate. You can paint, decoupage or leave the box au naturale and line with colored tissue paper. Add your cheese ball and tie with a ribbon.

Place your cheese ball in a small porcelain soufflé dish. Use cellophane to wrap, tie with a piece of raffia and slide a sprig of holly under the bow to complete your gift.

Shape your cheese recipe into a log shape. Place it on a small cutting board, and add a decorative cheese knife. Center the board on a large square of cellophane, bring the corners up and tie with decorative ribbon.

If you're making a selection of flavored cheese ball recipes, make mini balls and wrap individually in plastic film. Use self-adhesive stickers to indicate the type of each ball. Use an oblong serving plate, small wooden tray or oval au gratin dish to hold several cheese balls. Use a pretty tea towel to tie it all up in the Japanese furoshiki style of cloth wrapping. This makes a gift that will be used and appreciated for years.

Make mini truffle-sized cheese balls in an assortment of flavors and coatings. Fill an inexpensive serving plate with the tasty morsels and tie up with cellophane and a ribbon. Your recipient has an instant hors d'oeuvres tray that's ready to serve.

Cheese Roll

2 cups shredded Cheddar cheese
1/2 cup crumbled blue cheese
1 tablespoon grated onion
1 tablespoon milk
Parsley
Cooked crumbled bacon
Chopped nuts

Beat cheese until smooth, add milk and onion. On waxed paper, roll cheese into log form, roll in bacon, nuts, and parsley. Wrap and refrigerate.

Yield: 1 1/2 cups

Festive Cheese Ball

1 package cream cheese, 8 ounces
1 package blue cheese, 4 ounces
1 jar sharp cheddar cheese spread, 4 ounces
1/2 cup butter, melted
2/3 stuffed olives, chopped
1 tablespoon minced onions
Walnuts, finely chopped

Combine and mix well the three cheeses. Add hot melted butter. Blend in olives and onions. Chill. Roll into one large or 2 small balls. Roll in finely chopped walnuts or finely chopped parsley.

Cheese Ball

1 package cream cheese, 8 ounces
1 tablespoon toasted sesame seeds
2 tablespoons soy sauce

Roll cream cheese into a ball, roll in sesame seeds and sprinkle soy sauce on top. Spread on crackers.

Microwave Butter Crunch

5 tablespoons butter
1/2 teaspoon salt
6 cups any type of Chex® cereal
1/3 cups grated parmesan cheese

Melt the butter in a large bowl in the microwave for 50 to 60 seconds on high. Stir in the salt. Add the Chex® and stir to coat all pieces. Microwave on high 2 to 3 minutes until Chex is lightly toasted, stirring every half minute. Sprinkle the cheese on top of the Chex® mixture. Stir to coat all pieces. Spread on wax or parchment paper to cool.

Yield: 6 cups

Pineapple-Cheese Ball

2 cups pecans, finely chopped
1/4 green pepper, finely chopped
1/4 onion, finely chopped
2 packages cream cheese, 8 ounces each
1 can crushed pineapple, 8 ounces, well drained
1 teaspoon seasoned salt

Soften the cream cheese in microwave. Mix the chopped green pepper and onion together and add cream cheese; mix until smooth. Add pineapple, seasoned salt, and 1 cup chopped pecans. Mix well. Refrigerate mixture 1 hour; form into a ball and roll in remaining chopped pecans.

Cheese Olive Ball

Cream cheese, 8 ounces
1/3 cup butter
8 ounces shredded cheddar cheese
3/4 cup green olives, chopped
1/4 cup onion, chopped
1/2 cup nuts, crushed

Bring cream cheese, butter and shredded cheddar cheese to room temperature. Mix together well. Add olives and onions, then shape into a ball. Roll in nuts to cover ball. Refrigerate for 2 hours, stored in waxed paper.

Cheese Ball

Cream cheese, 6 ounces
Cheddar cheese, 3 ounces
Roquefort cheese, 3 ounces
1 tablespoon Worcestershire sauce
1/4 teaspoon onion salt
Walnuts or pecans, chopped

Bring the 3 cheeses to room temperature. Mix all ingredients together. Form into ball and roll in walnuts or pecans. Refrigerate until solid.

Blue Cheese Ball

Kraft® Old English cheddar cheese spread
Cream cheese, 8 ounces
Blue cheese, 2 ounces
1 teaspoon Worcestershire sauce
1 tablespoon chopped onions
10 green stuffed olives, chopped
Pecans, chopped

Mix all ingredients. Shape into a ball and roll in chopped pecans and parsley. Refrigerate until solid.

Pineapple Cheese Ball

1 can crushed pineapple, 8 ounces
2 packages cream cheese, 8 ounces each, softened
1 tablespoon seasoned salt
1/4 cup green pepper, finely chopped
2 cups chopped pecans

Beat the cream cheese till very smooth – mix in just one cup of pecans and the rest of the ingredients. Shape the mixture into a ball and roll in the final cup of pecans. Wrap in foil or plastic wrap and refrigerate until firm.

Yield: 40 appetizer servings

Easy Cheese Ball

Cream cheese, 8 ounce
1 10 ounce package sharp cheddar cheese spread
1 cup chopped pecans

Let cheeses soften. Mix cheeses together; form ball and roll in chopped pecans. Refrigerate until firm.

Easy Cheese Ball Wrapping

Wrap the cheese ball in plastic wrap. Center the cheese ball in a length of shrink wrap. Gather the top of the wrap and use a small rubber band to hold the shrink wrap upright. Use a hair dryer to shrink the wrap according to manufacturer's directions. Only shrink the wrap beneath the rubber band, leaving the excess wrap above the rubber band alone. Cut top to desired length. Add a red raffia bow. Place cheese ball in a basket with fruit and crackers.

Deviled Pecan Ball

2 packages cream cheese, 8 ounces each, softened
2 cups sharp cheddar cheese, shredded
1 can deviled ham, 2 1/4 ounces
2 teaspoons pimentos, chopped
2 to 4 drops hot sauce
2 teaspoons Worcestershire sauce
2 teaspoons grated onion
1 teaspoon dried parsley flakes
1 teaspoon lemon juice
1 teaspoon dry mustard
1/4 teaspoon seasoned salt
3/4 teaspoon paprika
2 cups chopped pecans

Combine the cream cheese, cheddar cheese and ham, blending well. Stir in remaining ingredients except pecans. Refrigerate for 2 hours. Divide cheese mixture in half and shape into 2 balls; roll in chopped pecans.

Dips

What's a party without some fabulous dips? Whether you prefer a flavorful seafood dip, a spicy veggie spread or a delicious dip to serve with fruit, we've collected the best party dip recipes for a smorgasbord of savory delights. Whether you are taking a dip to a party or giving it as a gift, make sure to include instructions if the recipe needs to be chilled, heated or otherwise prepared for serving.

Prepare Your Dipping Delights For Fuss Free Entertaining

Dips made with sour cream, cheese or dairy products will stay fresh in your refrigerator for three to four days, so you can prepare them well in advance. However, most dips don't do well in the freezer.

Chop, grind or cut your ingredients finely, so they are easy to scoop onto the crackers, fruits and vegetables.

Make sure you use only the freshest of fruits and vegetables in your dip recipe. Old, tired vegetables break down more quickly and rapidly become soggy and watery.

If you're taking your gift to a party, make your dip ahead of time to allow the flavors to blend.

Cool Containers For Party Dip

If you're contributing a dip to a party, use a unique bowl that's sure to get a second glance. Of course, you can hollow out a round loaf of French bread, but there are many other unique ideas that you can use.

Use a container that complements the dip ingredients. You can clean and hollow out a small pumpkin or melon. Scoop out an orange or grapefruit. Use a red or green cabbage or a head of lettuce to create a hollow bowl. Make sure to cut the bottom so it lies flat, but make sure the core still holds the leaves in place.

You can use any number of vegetables or fruits that have a hard outer rind. Use the contents you have removed from your bowl as ingredients for a stew or casserole.

Dip Containers That Keep On Giving

You can present your dip in a jumbo coffee mug. Tie it up with a square of cellophane and a bright raffia ribbon.

Use a pint mason jar as a gift container. Cut a square of fabric to cover the lid and secure with a rubber band. Tie a length of ribbon, twine, cord or raffia around the rubber band, finish with a bow and hang tag that lists the type of dip as well as the person's name.

Fill an earthenware crock with party dip. Cover the top with plastic wrap and secure in place with a rubber band. Place on a square of cellophane, draw up the four corners and tie with a colorful ribbon.

Pumpkin Dip

2 jars marshmallow crème, 7 ounces each
1 can pure pumpkin, 15 ounces (not pie filling)
1 cream cheese package, 8 ounces
1 teaspoon cinnamon
1 teaspoon pumpkin pie spice

Soften the cream cheese in microwave. Mix the cream cheese with the pumpkin, then fold in the marshmallow crème. Add the cinnamon and pumpkin pie spice. Store in refrigerator.

Pumpkin Dip

Serve this delicious dip in a hollowed out baby pumpkin with gingersnaps or molasses cookies, even apple slices.

Spicy Dip

1 pound Velveeta® cheese
1 pound American cheese
1 small can green chilies
1 small can taco sauce
1 small can stewed tomatoes
1 small jar salad olives

Melt cheese in microwave. Add all other ingredients. Keep warm. Serve with Doritos.

6 Layer Mexican Dip

1 can refried beans
1 container prepared guacamole
Sour cream, 8 ounces
1 large tomato, diced
1 can black olives, sliced
Cheddar cheese, 8 ounces, shredded

Layer all 6 ingredients in a round casserole dish. Refrigerate and serve with tortilla chips.

Cream Cheese Dip

1 small can crushed pineapple in heavy syrup
2 8 ounce packages cream cheese
2 teaspoons onions, chopped
1 cup green pepper, chopped
1 cup pecans, chopped
Lawry's® seasoning salt

Drain the pineapple and save juice. Combine pineapple, cream cheese, onions, green peppers and pecans. Season to taste with Lawry's® seasoning salt. Add the pineapple juice and mix. Refrigerate and serve with Wheat Thins®.

Overnight Vegetable Dip

1 cup dairy sour cream
1 1/2 cup mayonnaise
1/4 teaspoon tabasco sauce
1 cup onion, chopped
1 cup green pepper, chopped
1/4 teaspoon garlic salt
2 teaspoons salt
1/2 teaspoon pepper

Mix all ingredients together. Refrigerate overnight in covered container.

Yield: 4 cups

French Veggie Dip

Cream cheese, 8 ounces
1/2 package Good Seasons® French Salad Dressing mix (dry)
1/3 cup tomato juice
8 drops of hot sauce
1/4 cup diced onions

Soften cream cheese in microwave. Add all ingredients to cream cheese, mix well. Refrigerate.

Spinach Dip

Package frozen chopped spinach, 10 ounces
1 1/2 cups mayonnaise
1/4 to 1/2 cup chopped onions
Salt and pepper

Thaw spinach and squeeze out water. Mix all ingredients. Refrigerate.

Vegetable Dip

Sour cream, 16 ounces
3/4 cup mayonnaise
3 tablespoons minced onion
1 tablespoon beau monde seasoning
3 tablespoons parsley flakes
1 tablespoon dill weed

Mix all ingredients together. Refrigerate.

(To make your own beau monde seasoning:

Mix 1 teaspoon each of the following: cinnamon, nutmeg, celery seed, mace with 1 tablespoon each of the following: white pepper, allspice, ground bay leaf, salt, ground cloves and 2 tablespoons black pepper)

Spicy Cheese Dip

1 pound Velveeta® cheese, 16 ounces
1 medium can Rotel® tomatoes, 10 ounces
Small Owens® sausage – mild, 1/2 pound

Cook the sausage. Cut the cheese into chunks for quicker melting. Melt cheese with tomatoes in slow cooker. Add sausage.

This can also be made in the microwave. Just combine the cheese, tomatoes and cooked sausage until the cheese is melted, stirring about every minute.

Serve with Doritos®.

Pistachio Dip For Fruit Kabobs

2 packages cream cheese, 8 ounces each
1 jar marshmallow creme, 7 ounces
4 teaspoons lime juice
2 tablespoons pistachio nuts, finely chopped
Fruit such as seedless grapes (red or green), melon, pineapple

Combine the cream cheese, marshmallow creme, lime juice and pistachio nuts; chill. For kabobs, use 3 pieces of fruit on 4 inch skewers. Two seedless grapes with a 3/4 inch cube of melon, pineapple, etc. in the middle is good. Use a grape on the pointed end of the skewer; other fruits tend to fall into the dip.

To serve, place dip in small bowl in the center of a round tray; arrange kabobs in a circle around the dip.

Makes enough dip for 96 Kabobs.

Pecan Dip

2 teaspoons butter
1/2 teaspoon salt
1/2 cup pecans
8 ounce package cream cheese, softened
2 1/2 ounce jar dried beef
2 teaspoons milk
1/4 cup green pepper, chopped
1/4 teaspoon pepper
1/2 teaspoon garlic salt
1/2 cup sour cream
Small onion, chopped

Melt butter in skillet over medium heat, then add salt. Toast pecans in butter for about 10 minutes, stirring frequently. Mix in the rest of the ingredients. Butter an 8" pie pan. Put the mixture in the pan and arrange pecans on top. Bake at 350 degrees F for 20 minutes. Serve hot with crackers.

Holiday Shrimp Dip

Cream cheese, 8 ounces
1/2 cup Heinz® chili sauce
2 teaspoons horseradish
1/2 cup mayonnaise
1/4 cup onion, chopped
Package tiny shrimp, 4 1/2 ounces, rinsed and drained

Soften the cream cheese in the microwave. Mix the chili sauce and cream cheese. Add the horseradish, mayonnaise and onion. Mix in the shrimp. Refrigerate for at least one hour.

Reuben Dip

2 packages corned beef, 2.5 ounce each
16 ounce can sauerkraut rinsed and drained
1 cup Thousand Island dressing
8 ounces Swiss cheese, shredded

Cut the corned beef into small pieces. Mix the beef, sauerkraut, dressing and cheese together. Microwave 8 to 10 minutes until hot.

Smoked Oyster Dip

1 3 1/4 ounce jar of smoked oysters
3 ounce package cream cheese
1 tablespoon milk
1/4 cup mayonnaise
1/4 teaspoon salt
1/2 teaspoon seasoned salt
1/8 teaspoon pepper
2 teaspoons lemon juice

Soften the cream cheese in the microwave. Stir the milk, mayonnaise, salts, pepper and lemon juice in with the cream cheese. Chop the oysters and gently mix them into the cream cheese mixture. Refrigerate and serve with crackers.

Smoked Fish Dip

1/2 cup mayonnaise
1 cup sour cream
2 cups smoked fish, flaked
4 tablespoons green onion, chopped
3/4 teaspoon Worcestershire sauce
1 teaspoon garlic powder

In a bowl, mix mayonnaise and sour cream. Stir in fish, onion, Worcestershire sauce and garlic powder. Cover and refrigerate at least 1 hour.

Yield: 1 1/2 cups

Cheesecake Dip

Cream cheese, 8 ounces, softened
4 teaspoons sugar
6 teaspoons milk
4 cups Cool Whip®
2 teaspoons vanilla

Beat with mixer the cheese, sugar, milk and vanilla until well blended and free from lumps. Fold in the Cool Whip®. Store in refrigerator. Use to dip fresh fruit, cake cubes, pretzel sticks, etc.

Variation: Use the flavored Neufchatel cheeses, such as orange, berry, etc.

Cheesecake Dip in a Gift Jar

Gifts from your kitchen are always welcome during the holidays. Add this dip jar to a basket of fruit. The label can be printed at www.NorthPoleChristmas.com/holiday.html

Dill Dip

2/3 cup mayonnaise
2/3 cup sour cream
1 teaspoon dry onion flakes
1 teaspoon dill weed
2 teaspoons garlic salt
1 teaspoon parsley flakes

Mix all ingredients together and refrigerate for several hours. Serve with raw vegetables.

Spicy Cranberry Dip

1 can jellied cranberry sauce, 16 ounces
2 teaspoons honey
3 teaspoons prepared horseradish
1 teaspoon lemon juice
1 teaspoon Worcestershire sauce
1 clove garlic minced
1/2 teaspoon ground red pepper

In a medium saucepan, combine all ingredients. Bring to boiling; reduce heat. Simmer, covered, about 5 minutes. Serve warm with orange pieces, pineapple chunks and smoked turkey link sausage.

Layered Bean Dip

1 can black beans, 15 ounces, rinsed and drained
1 can refried beans, 16 ounces
1/2 cup sour cream
1 cup cheddar cheese, shredded
1 cup bottled salsa
Cilantro, chopped

Preheat oven to 375 degrees F. In a bowl, combine the two beans. Spread the bean mixture in an 8 or 9" square baking dish. Spread the sour cream over the bean mixture, top with cheese and salsa. Cover with tin foil and bake for 20 minutes. Uncover and bake 10 minutes more or until bubbly. Garnish with cilantro.

Hot Crab Dip

Cream cheese, 8 ounces
1/2 cup margarine
1 lb. crab meat, chopped

Cut cream cheese in pieces. Place in microwave dish along with margarine and chopped crab meat. Microwave all ingredients together for 2 to 3 minutes.

California Dip

1 small can black olives, chopped
1 small can green chilies, chopped and drained
3 large fresh ripe tomatoes, chopped and drained
3 green onions and tops, chopped
1 teaspoon garlic salt
1/2 teaspoon salt
Pepper to taste
3 teaspoons olive oil
1 1/2 teaspoon red wine vinegar

Combine olives, chilies, tomatoes, onion, salts, pepper, oil and vinegar. Serve with tortilla chips.

Cakes

If you've primed your taste buds for cake, why not indulge yourself with a new recipe. From the traditional fruit cake, a decadent Cranberry Cake with Hot Butter Sauce and a ready-in-a-flash Pulitzer Pudding Cake, we've collected some of the tastiest, never-fail desserts to make a perfect ending to your holiday feasts.

Tips To Make Your Cake A Hit

For the holidays, you can bake cake recipes in a Bundt pan for an extra special look. You don't have to adjust the ingredients, but allow extra time for cooking. Most Bundt cake recipes require 45 to 60 minutes baking time at 350 degrees Fahrenheit. When the cake begins to pull away from the sides, insert a toothpick to check for doneness. If the cake is still too moist in the center, allow another five minutes and check again. When the cake is cooled, drizzle with your favorite icing that has been thinned to a pouring consistency. Add a sprig of holly, a decorative tree ornament or plastic snowflake as a festive embellishment.

If you would like to make mini cakes, there are cute mini cake pans, mini Bundt pans and other unusual shaped bakeware available. Mini cakes will take less baking time, so reduce the cooking time by one-half of the recommended recipe time and check for doneness every five minutes thereafter.

Add a tablespoon or two of meringue powder to your cake batter. This lightens the texture of your cake and it will rise a bit higher.

A teaspoon of lemon juice added before creaming the butter and sugar produces a lighter cake texture.

After greasing your pan, use cocoa powder instead of flour to dust your pan when making a chocolate cake.

Place a pan of water in the oven when baking a fruitcake or other dense recipe. This keeps your cake moist.

Put your hand in a plastic bag when greasing a cake pan.

Cut a piece of wax paper to fit the bottom of your pan. After greasing the bottom, set the paper in place and grease the paper insert.

To remove layer cakes from the pans, allow the cake to cool completely on a wire rack before removing. Run a knife along the edge to loosen before turning the pan over.

Fruit Cake

1 1/2 cup Brazil nuts (1 pound), unshelled or other nuts of your choice
1 1/2 cup walnuts
2/3 cup candied orange peel
1 package pitted dates, 7 ounces
1/2 cup raisins (brown or golden)
1/2 cup maraschino red cherries (whole)
1/2 cup maraschino green cherries (whole)
3/4 cup flour
1/2 teaspoon salt
3/4 cup sugar
1/2 teaspoon baking powder
3 eggs
1 teaspoon vanilla

Put fruit and nuts in large bowl. Put flour, sugar, salt and baking powder over nuts and fruit. Beat eggs. Add vanilla and pour over fruit and nut mixture, stirring until mixed well. Bake in greased, wax paper lined pan (5x10x3" or small size) at 300 degrees for 1 3/4 hours. May be baked in smaller pans, but time may have to be adjusted.

Yield: 3 pounds

Popcorn Cake

20 cups popped corn
1 pound cashews or peanuts, unshelled
1 pound red and green gum drops
1 package miniature marshmallows
1/2 cup oil
1/2 cup butter

Melt marshmallows, oil and butter in double boiler (or microwave). Place popcorn, nuts and gumdrops in large bowl. Pour melted mixture over dry ingredients. Mix and press into buttered angel food pans.

Pumpkin Cream Cake

3 eggs
1 cup sugar
1 teaspoon lemon juice
2/3 cup solid-pack pumpkin
3/4 cup flour
1 teaspoon baking powder
1 1/2 teaspoon pumpkin pie spice
2 teaspoons cinnamon
1/2 teaspoon salt
1 cup nuts
Powdered sugar for rolling

Beat eggs on high speed for exactly 5 minutes. Add sugar to eggs and mix. Add the lemon juice and pumpkin. In a bowl, combine the flour, baking powder, cinnamon, pumpkin pie spice and salt. Add to egg mixture. Spread out on a greased cookie sheet. Sprinkle the nuts on the batter. Bake at 375 degrees F for 15 minutes. Let cool in pan for 10 minutes. Take cake from pan and put on a cloth towel that has been heavily sprinkled with powdered sugar and some nuts. Roll the cake up with the towel in it and let cool.

Filling:

1 large package cream cheese, room temperature
4 tablespoons margarine, softened
1 cup powdered sugar
1 teaspoon vanilla

Meanwhile, mix together, the cream cheese, margarine, sugar and vanilla for the filling. Unroll the cake. Spread the cream cheese mixture on the cake and re-roll. Refrigerate.

Mini-Cream Cheese Cupcakes

1 cup sugar
1 1/2 cups flour
1/3 cup cocoa
1 cup water
1 tablespoon vinegar
1/2 cup salad oil
1 teaspoon baking soda
1 teaspoon vanilla

Filling:
Cream cheese, 8 ounces
1 egg
1/3 cup sugar
Chocolate chips, 6 ounces

Combine cream cheese, egg and sugar and mix with electric mixer to make the cream cheese filling. Stir in chocolate chips. In a separate large bowl, combine the rest of the ingredients to make the chocolate cake mixture. Beat until smooth.

Fill cupcake pans half full of the chocolate cake mixture. Top with the cream cheese filling. Bake in a 350 degrees oven for 16 to 17 minutes if using mini-cupcake pans, or 22 minutes if using regular cupcake pans.

Pumpkin Delight

1 yellow cake mix
1 cup butter, melted, divided
3 eggs, divided
2 cans pumpkin
2/3 cup evaporated milk
1/2 cup white sugar
1 teaspoon cinnamon

Preheat oven to 350 degrees F. Set aside 1 cup of the dry cake mix. Mix the rest of the cake mix, one beaten egg and 1/2 cup of the melted butter. Mix well, press into the bottom of a greased 9 x 13 pan.

Mix together pumpkin, evaporated milk, and 2 eggs. Pour this over the crust. Combine the cup of cake mix that was set aside with the sugar and the remaining 1/2 cup of melted butter; add cinnamon. Mix well. Drop by spoonfuls over the top of pumpkin mixture. Bake for 45 minutes or until done. Cut into squares and serve with whipped cream.

Apple Strudel Cake

2 cups sugar
1 cup vegetable oil
2 eggs, beaten
2 1/2 cups flour
3 cups tart apples, chopped
1 cup pecans, broken
1 teaspoon cinnamon
1 teaspoon vanilla
Butterscotch chips, 6 ounces

Mix sugar, oil and eggs; beat well. Add apples and mix to blend. Add flour and beat until it is blended in; stir in nuts, cinnamon and vanilla. Batter will be stiff. Spread in a 13x9 inch baking pan that has been greased and floured. Sprinkle butterscotch chips on top and bake at 350 degrees F for 50 minutes.

Fruit Cocktail Cake

2 cups flour
1 1/2 cups sugar
1/4 teaspoon salt
2 teaspoons baking soda
1 can fruit cocktail, 17 oz. (save juice)
2 eggs, beaten
1/2 cup brown sugar
1/2 cup walnuts

In a bowl, combine the flour, sugar, baking soda and salt. Pour fruit cocktail plus juice in the bowl. Add the eggs. Mix and pour in greased and floured large cake pan. Sprinkle top with brown sugar and walnuts. Bake at 350° for 30 to 35 minutes. Cool, then frost.

Frosting:

3/4 cup margarine
3/4 cup sugar
3/4 cup Pet® evaporated milk
1 teaspoon vanilla
1 cup coconut

Combine the margarine, sugar and milk in a pan. Cook and after it has started to boil, stir constantly. Boil for 5 to 20 minutes or until it starts getting fairly thick. Take off stove and add 1 teaspoon vanilla and 1/2 to 1 cup of coconut. Pour over cake.

Cranberry Cake with Hot Butter Sauce

3 teaspoons butter, melted
1 cup sugar
1/2 cup water
1/2 cup Carnation® evaporated milk
2 cups flour
1 teaspoon salt
1 teaspoon baking soda
2 cups raw cranberries

Mix butter, sugar, milk and water together. Add the flour, salt, baking soda and cranberries. Bake in an 8x8 inch pan for 30 to 40 minutes. Test middle with toothpick. Serve with hot butter sauce.

Sauce:

1/2 cup butter
1 cup sugar
1 teaspoon vanilla
1/2 cup Carnation® evaporated milk

Sauce – Mix all ingredients together in a saucepan and bring to boil. Serve over cranberry cake.

Peanuty Cupcakes

1/3 cup margarine
1/2 cup chunky peanut butter
1 1/2 cups brown sugar, packed
1 teaspoon vanilla
2 eggs
2 cups flour
2 teaspoons baking powder
1/2 teaspoon salt
1 cup milk

Cream margarine and peanut butter together. Add brown sugar and mix. Add eggs and vanilla and beating until airy. Add milk, flour, salt and baking powder and beat well. Fill paper baking cups in muffin pans half full. Bake at 375 degrees F for 15 to 20 minutes. Cool. Frost with Peanut Butter Glaze.

Peanut Butter Glaze:

1 cup peanut butter
1/2 cup margarine
2 cups confectioners' sugar
3 tablespoons of milk

Beat the peanut butter and margarine together with mixer. Add the sugar and milk and mix well. Add more milk if needed for spreading.

Cinnamon Cheese Bars

2 packages crescent rolls
2 packages cream cheese, 8 ounces each
1 egg, separated
1 cup sugar

Spread 1 package crescent rolls in greased 9 x 13 inch pan. Soften cream cheese in microwave; add 1 cup sugar and egg yolk. Spread on top of crust. Cover with remaining tube of rolls. Froth egg white and brush on top.

Add topping:

1/2 cup sugar
1/2 cup chopped nuts
1 teaspoon cinnamon

Bake at 350 degrees F for 20 to 25 minutes.

Pulitzer Pudding Cake

1 can fruit pie filling (any flavor)
1 layer size box cake mix (or use 1/2 of a regular cake mix box)
1 cup nuts, chopped
1/2 cup butter

Pour the fruit pie filling in a 9 inch pie pan. Sprinkle the dry cake mix evenly over the pie filling. Sprinkle with nuts. Dot with small pieces of butter. Bake at 350 degrees F for 45 minutes.

Cherry Kuchen

1/2 cup butter
1/4 cup sugar
1 egg yolk
1 1/4 cups flour
1 teaspoon salt

Cream butter, sugar and egg yolk together with a spoon. Add flour and salt and mix well. Pat into a 9 x 13" pan, working up the sides. Combine 1 tablespoon sugar and 1 tablespoon flour and sprinkle on crust.

Filling:

1 can sour cherries
3 tablespoons cornstarch

Drain the cherries juice into a small saucepan and set aside. Add the 3 tablespoons of cornstarch to a little water. Add 1/2 cup of sugar to the cherries juice, and add the cornstarch and water mixture. Cook the juice over medium heat until thick. Remove from heat and mix the can of cherries in with the juice. Put the cherries with the thickened juice in crust.

Topping:

3/4 cup sugar
2 tablespoons cream
2 eggs, beaten

Mix all the topping ingredients and pour over cherries. Bake at 350 degrees F for 20 minutes, then lower oven to 325 degrees F for 30 minutes longer. Serve with whipped cream.

Appetizers

Whether you're the host or contributing a tray of goodies to the next holiday get-together, a savory and substantial tray of appetizers will please a hungry horde.

Recipes that can be served at room temperature are great for your hostess, but you can bring your warm dish in a slow cooker that can be set up on the buffet and plugged in to keep warm for hours.

Stuffed Mushrooms

12 long or 24 medium mushrooms
1 teaspoon onions with tops, minced
2 teaspoons butter
1 can crab meat, 6 1/2 ounces, rinsed and drained
1/2 cup pitted ripe olives, diced
1/4 cup fine dry bread crumbs
2 teaspoons mayonnaise
2 teaspoons lemon juice
1 teaspoon butter

Heat oven to 375 degrees F. Remove stems from mushrooms; chop stems. Sauté chopped mushrooms stems and the onions in 2 teaspoons butter about 5 minutes until onions are tender. Combine sautéed mixture and remaining ingredients except 1 teaspoon butter. Stuff mushroom caps with crab mixture mounding tops. Dot equally with 1 teaspoon butter. Bake in well-buttered 9 inch square dish until filling is hot, about 15 minutes.

Yield: 12 servings

Buffalo Wings

3/4 cup cider vinegar
1/4 cup lemon juice
2 teaspoons vegetable oil
1 teaspoon Worcestershire sauce
1 teaspoon garlic, minced
1 to 2 teaspoons hot sauce or more
1 teaspoon celery salt
2 teaspoons sugar
1 teaspoon ground cumin
1 teaspoon ground pepper
1/2 teaspoon ground red pepper
4 pounds chicken wings

Combine all ingredients and pour over cleaned chicken wings in jumbo Ziploc bag. Marinate overnight, turning bag occasionally. Bake on lined jelly roll pan at 350 degrees F for approximately 1 hour until browned and cooked through.

Serve with Bleu Cheese dressing for dipping.

Chicken Bites

2 pounds boneless chicken breasts
3 cups Pepperidge Farm® Herb Seasoned Stuffing
3 tablespoons orange juice
Honey mustard salad dressing, 18 ounces

Cut the chicken breasts into 1 inch pieces. Pour one cup of salad dressing in a bowl and dip the chicken in the dressing. Crush the stuffing into small pieces, put it on a plate and roll the chicken in the stuffing.

Use 2 cookie sheets for the chicken and bake at 400 degrees F for 15 minutes or until the chicken is done. Mix the orange juice and remaining salad dressing in a saucepan and heat over medium heat. Serve the hot dressing mixture with the chicken for dipping.

Cheesy Bake Appetizers

Sharp cheddar cheese, 6 ounces, grated
Monterey Jack cheese, 8 ounces, grated
Green chili peppers, 4 ounce can, drained
1 cup mayonnaise
1/4 teaspoon garlic powder
1 baguette (French bread or sour dough)

Slice baguette into 1/2" slices. Combine mayonnaise and cheese. Add garlic powder and green chili and mix with a spoon. Spread mixture on baguette slices. (Slices may be frozen and baked later.) Place on cookie sheets. Bake at 350 degrees for 15 minutes until slices are brown and bubbly.

Sausage Cheese Balls

2 packages uncooked breakfast sausage
4 cups sharp cheddar cheese, shredded
1 1/2 cups Bisquick®
1/2 cup onion, finely chopped
1/2 cup celery, finely chopped
1/2 teaspoon garlic powder

Preheat oven to 375 degrees F. Mix all ingredients and roll into 1 inch balls. Bake 15 minutes on ungreased baking sheet until brown.

Best Teriyaki Chicken Wings

3 to 6 pounds of chicken wings
1/4 cup pineapple juice
1 cup water
1 cup soy sauce
1/4 cup oil
1 cup brown sugar
1 teaspoon garlic
1 teaspoon ginger

If using whole chicken wings, cut sections apart and discard tips. Mix water, soy sauce, pineapple juice, oil, brown sugar, garlic and ginger. Pour over chicken wings. Marinate in refrigerator overnight. Bake wings and sauce at 350 degrees F in a large pan until sauce is caramelized about 60 to 90 minutes. Baked wings may be kept warm or served in a crock pot.

Hot Cheese And Chili Spread

2 cans chopped chilies drained
1 bar Cracker Barrel® sharp cheese, shredded
1 egg
1 teaspoon milk

Put the drained chilies in the bottom of a 9 inch pie plate. Mix cheese, egg, and milk together; spread over the chilies. Shake paprika on top. Bake in a 350 degrees F oven for 20 minutes, until bubbly.

Serve with Doritos.

Drinks

Whether you want to celebrate Christmas with a traditional Wassail or warm up after a vigorous snowball fight with Snowmobiler's Apple Cider, we've scoured our recipes for the tastiest and easiest entertaining drinks. Cool and refreshing or warm and creamy, there's something to please everyone with this delightful compilation of holiday drinks.

Christmas Wassail

1 gallon apple cider
1 orange, peeled and sliced
4 cinnamon sticks, 3" each
2 teaspoons grated orange zest
1/2 teaspoon ground ginger
1/2 teaspoon grated nutmeg

Combine ingredients over low heat. Simmer. Serve warm.

Yield: 16 servings

Spiced Tea

1/2 cup instant tea
1 to 2 cups sugar
2 cups instant orange drink powder (like Tang®)
2 teaspoons cinnamon

Combine all ingredients and store in airtight container. To serve, stir in 1 1/2 teaspoons into one cup of water.

Holiday Eggnog

1/4 cup sugar
1/4 teaspoon ginger
1/4 teaspoon cinnamon
1/4 teaspoon ground cloves
6 eggs, well beaten
1/2 cup lemon juice, cold
2 quarts orange juice, cold
1 quart ginger ale, cold
1 quart vanilla ice cream
Ground nutmeg

In a bowl, beat eggs with sugar, ginger, cinnamon and cloves. Stir in the orange and lemon juice. Cut vanilla ice cream into pieces and place in a large bowl. Gradually pour in the ginger ale. Sprinkle the eggnog with ground nutmeg.

Yield: 20 servings.

Mulled Cider

2 quarts sweet apple juice
20 whole cloves
1/2 cup sugar
12 sticks cinnamon
14 whole allspices
1/4 teaspoon salt

Combine all ingredients together in order. Heat to boiling. Simmer 15 minutes. Allow to stand 12 hours. Strain and serve hot.

Yield: 8 servings

Hot Cranberry Christmas Punch

3 cups whole fresh cranberries
3 1/2 quarts water
12 whole cloves
4 whole cinnamon sticks
4 lemons, juiced
4 oranges, juiced
2 cups sugar

In a large pot, combine cranberries, cinnamon, cloves and water. Bring mixture to a boil. Cover and reduce heat, simmering for 12 minutes. Strain juice and return to kettle. Add the juice of the lemons and oranges; add sugar. Stir until sugar dissolves. Serve hot.

Spiced Apple Cider

2 quarts apple cider
1 1/2 cups orange juice
1 teaspoon coriander
1 teaspoon allspice
1 cinnamon stick
1/4 cup brown sugar

Simmer 10-15 minutes. Strain and warm or cool and serve cool.

New England Eggnog

6 eggs, separated
1 cup sugar
3 cups heavy cream
3 cups milk
1 1/2 cup light rum
3/4 cup peach brandy
3/4 teaspoon nutmeg
Dash of salt

Beat egg yolks, adding sugar gradually, until light and fluffy. Slowly add cream, milk, brandy and rum. Refrigerate. Just before serving, beat egg whites and salt until stiff. Fold into eggnog and sprinkle with nutmeg.

Serves 12.

Spiced Fruit Punch

1/2 cup sugar
12 cloves
1 1/2 cups water
4 sticks of cinnamon
1/2 cup lemon juice
1 1/2 cups orange juice
1 can pineapple juice, 46 ounces

Simmer sugar, cloves, water and cinnamon for 30 minutes. Strain and add to fruit juices. Chill. Pour over ice or frozen pineapple juice cubes. Makes 2 quarts.

Snowmobiler's Apple Cider

1 gallon apple cider
1 small can frozen orange juice

Place in large coffee maker.

In basket put:

3 to 4 sticks cinnamon
6 to 9 whole cloves
1 cup brown sugar

Heat as you would coffee. Serve hot.

Salads

Salads for holiday buffets and parties should be fun, festive and a little decadent. You've had enough healthy greens and now it's time to treat your family and friends with rich, flavorful and unusual salads that will make a welcome addition to the holiday dinner table. Fruits, whipped toppings, cheeses and nuts transform plain gelatin into a colorful and delicious treat that's great for lunch buffets or sit down dinners.

Cherry Coke Jell-O® Salad

1 large box cherry Jell-O®
1 cup boiling water
1 15 ounce can crushed pineapple, drained
1 can cherry Coke®
Chopped nuts
1 can cherry pie filling

Mix the Jell-O® and boiling water until Jell-O® is dissolved. Add pineapple, Coke, pie filling and nuts. Mix well. Stir a couple of times as it is setting. Refrigerate until firm.

Red Cinnamon Apple Salad

2/3 cup red hot cinnamon candies
1 cup hot water
1 3 ounce package lemon Jell-O®
1 1/2 cup applesauce

Pour hot water over red hot candies and stir until dissolved. Add package of lemon Jell-O® and stir until dissolved. Add applesauce and pour entire mixture into a baking pan or Jell-O® mold. Chill in refrigerator until firm.

Yield: 6 servings

Holiday Salad

1 can Eagle Brand® milk
1 can cherry pie filling
1 large can pineapple, crushed, drained
9 ounce Cool Whip®
1 1/2 cup mini-marshmallows
1/2 to 1 cup walnuts to put on top

Mix all together in order listed. Put in refrigerator overnight. Spread walnuts on top.

Pistachio Salad

1 box pistachio instant pudding mix, 3 3/4 ounces
1/3 cup milk
1 carton frozen whipped topping, 13 ounce
1 can crushed pineapple, 8 ounces, drained
1 cup miniature marshmallows

Mix pudding and milk, fold in whipped topping, pineapple and marshmallows. Mix ingredients well. Allow to set in refrigerator.

Triple Orange Salad

2 packages orange jello, 3 ounces each
2 cups boiling water
2 1/2 cups crushed pineapple
Can of mandarin oranges, 11 ounces
Pint of orange sherbet

Dissolve jello in water and add the sherbet, pineapple and oranges. Refrigerate.

Holiday Jell-O Salad

1 cup crushed pineapple
1/2 cup cheddar cheese
1 cup pecans, chopped
1 medium carton Cool Whip®
1 cup sugar
Large orange Jell-O®

Blend all ingredients together and refrigerate. It is better after it has set for several hours.

Substitutes: Dream Whip®, whipping cream. Cottage cheese can be added for texture or cream cheese to make it richer.

Fruity Orange Jell-O Mold

2 cups boiling water
2 packages orange Jell-O®, 3 ounces each
1 1/4 cups cold water
1 teaspoon orange juice
1 package cream cheese, 8 ounces, softened
1 can mandarin oranges, 11 ounces, drained
1 can crushed pineapple, 8 ounces, drained and diced

Dissolve Jell-O® in boiling water. Add cold water and orange juice. Measure 1 cup; pour into a 6 cup mold. Chill until set but not firm.

Blend remaining gelatin very slowly into cream cheese, beating until smooth. Place bowl of Jell-O® in a larger bowl of water and ice. Stir until thickened. Add fruits and pour into mold over clear gelatin. Chill until firm, about 4 hours. Unmold.

Yield: 6 cups or 12 servings

Snickers Salad

5 Snickers® candy bars cut into little pieces
8 granny smith apples, peeled and diced
1 large carton of Cool Whip®
1 large package instant vanilla pudding (dry)

Mix all ingredients together. Serve cold.

Caramel Apple Salad

8 small apples, diced
1 can crushed pineapple, 8 ounces, undrained
1 box butterscotch pudding (dry)
1/4 cup chopped nuts
Fat Free Cool Whip®, 8 ounces

Mix apples, pineapple with juice, butterscotch pudding and nuts. Mix well then fold in Cool Whip® and refrigerate.

Pineapple Salad

1 cup crushed pineapple, drained
1 cup pineapple juice
2 teaspoons cornstarch
1/2 cup sugar
2 eggs, beaten
1/2 cup shredded cheese
1 cup miniature marshmallows
1 cup nuts

Mix pineapple, cheese, marshmallows and nuts; set aside. In a saucepan, combine pineapple juice, cornstarch and sugar. Cook until thick and add eggs. Cook 2 minutes longer. Pour over the pineapple mixture and mix thoroughly. Refrigerate.

Blueberry Salad

2 small boxes grape Jell-O®
2 cups boiling water
1 can crushed pineapple, 20 ounces
1 can blueberry pie filling
1/2 cup sour cream
Cream cheese, 8 ounces, softened
1/2 cup sugar
1 teaspoon vanilla
1/2 cup chopped nuts

Boil water. Add Jell-O®, stirring until melted. Add pineapple (with juice) and pie filling. Put in bottom of clear bowl and chill until solid. In another bowl, whip together sour cream, cream cheese, sugar and vanilla. Spread over Jell-O® mix. Sprinkle on chopped pecans and chill again.

Cherry Red Salad

1 package cherry flavored gelatin, 3 ounce
1 package strawberry flavored gelatin, 3 ounce
1 can crushed pineapple, 16 ounces
1 can pitted Bing cherries, 16 ounces
3 packages cream cheese, 3 ounces each
1 can Coca-Cola®, 16 ounces
1 cup chopped nuts

Drain juices from fruits, adding water to make 2 cups. Heat to boiling. Pour over gelatins and stir until dissolved. Add fruit, cream cheese, nuts and Coke®. Mix well and pour into a greased 12 cups mold. Refrigerate.

Yield: 12 servings

Coconut Fruit Salad

3 1/2 cups Cool Whip®, thawed
2 cups miniature marshmallows
Fruit cocktail, 16 ounces, drained
Crushed pineapple, 8 ounces, drained
2 cups coconut
1/2 cup milk

Combine all ingredients and mix well. Refrigerate for at least one hour.

Yield: 6 cups or 12 servings

Christmas Fruit Salad

2 cans cherry pie filling
1 can sliced peaches, drained
1 can pineapple tidbits, drained
1 package frozen strawberries
2 bananas, sliced

Mix all of the above ingredients together. Add bananas just before serving.

Bars, Brownies and Muffins

Sometimes you need something fast, and bars, brownies and muffins fill the bill. Easy to assemble, quick to bake up and rich with flavor, bar recipes are on everyone's favorites list. Frosted or unfrosted, bars pack well and make a great last minute gift.

Bar Baking Basics

Line a baking pan with parchment paper before filling with batter. After baking, allow the pan to cool to room temperature. Do not cut the bars. Use the paper to lift the contents out of the baking pan. Now you can easily cut and separate the bars without damaging them, using a sharp knife.

Frosted bars should be iced after cutting into squares. That way you can remove crumbs and have perfectly frosted bars.

Muffin Magic Cooking Tips

For baking muffins, use five inch squares of parchment paper in place of cupcake liners for a unique, bakery-style look.

Mix dry ingredients in one bowl and wet ingredients in another. Make a depression in the dry ingredients and add the wet into the hole.

Do not over stir the batter. It should contain lumps and be stirred only enough to moisten all the ingredients. Overbeating can cause a tough texture.

To prevent nuts and fruits from sinking while baking, dust them with flour before adding to the batter. You can also toast the nuts before adding or sprinkle nuts on top of the batter after filling the pan.

Gift Packaging For Bars, Brownies And Muffins

If you have someone on your list that's moving into their first place, pack your bars into a baking pan. It could be a coated metal pan, ovenproof earthenware pan or a shiny steel baker's pan. Choose a size and shape that fits their needs. Wrap in colorful cellophane, tie it up with ribbon and add a hanging tag. You could also write or print out the recipe for your tasty treat.

In the same vein, wrap muffins individually and place in a cupcake pan. Tie the entire package in cellophane and add a ribbon with a bow.

Banana Chocolate Chip Muffins

2 bananas, extra ripe
2 eggs
1 cup brown sugar
1/2 cup butter, melted
1 teaspoon vanilla
2 1/4 cups flour
1/2 teaspoon cinnamon
1/2 teaspoon salt
2 teaspoons baking powder
1 cup chocolate chips
1/2 cup walnuts, chopped

Mash bananas. Blend in eggs, sugar, butter and vanilla. Combine the flour, cinnamon, salt and baking powder and make a well in the center. Pour in the banana mixture and mix just to blend. Stir in chocolate chips and nuts. Spoon into 12 well-greased 2 1/2 inch muffin pan cups or use mini muffin pans. Bake in 350 degrees F oven for 25 to 30 minutes.

Bag Toppers

Clear plastic cellophane bags that are 4" wide are available at craft stores. They work well for wrapping one or two large pieces of brownie. Visit NorthPoleChristmas.com/holiday.html to print the 4" bag toppers above and more.

Mint Brownies

Brownie:

1/2 cup butter
1 cup sugar
4 eggs
1 cup flour
Hershey's® chocolate syrup, 16 ounces

Preheat oven to 350 degrees F. Cream together butter and sugar. Add eggs, flour and Hershey's® syrup. Beat until smooth. Pour into 9 x 13" pan and bake for 25 to 30 minutes or until toothpick comes out clean. Top may appear wet. When completely cool, top with mint layer.

Mint Layer:

1/2 cup butter, softened
2 to 3 cups powdered sugar
4 teaspoon milk
1/2 teaspoon mint extract or peppermint extract
3 drops green food coloring

Cream butter and sugar. Add milk, extract and food coloring. Beat until smooth. Spread over brownie layer. Refrigerate until firm. Top with chocolate frosting.

Chocolate Frosting:

6 teaspoons butter
1 cup semi-sweet chocolate chips

Place butter and chips in small saucepan and melt slowly. Mix well and cool slightly, pour over mint layer. Keep brownies refrigerated.

Pumpkin Bars

1 2/3 cups sugar
1 cup oil
4 eggs
1 can of pumpkin, 16 oz.
1 teaspoon salt
2 cups flour
2 teaspoon cinnamon
2 teaspoon baking powder
1 teaspoon baking soda

In a bowl, beat the eggs, oil, pumpkin and sugar until fluffy. In a separate bowl, mix together flour, salt, cinnamon, baking powder and soda. Add the flour mixture to the pumpkin mix and combine thoroughly. Spread batter in ungreased 9x13" pan. Bake at 350° for 25 to 30 minutes. Cool and frost.

Pumpkin Bars Icing

1/2 cup butter, melted
1 package cream cheese, 3 oz., softened
2 cups powdered sugar
1 teaspoon vanilla

Cream the butter and cream cheese together. Stir in powdered sugar and vanilla a little at a time, beating until smooth.

Pineapple Brownies

3/4 cup margarine, melted
1 1/2 cups sugar
3 eggs
1 teaspoon vanilla
1 1/2 cups flour
1/2 teaspoon salt
1/3 teaspoon cinnamon
1 teaspoon baking powder
1 cup crushed pineapple, drained
2 squares chocolate, melted
1/2 cup nuts, chopped

Cream margarine and sugar together, then add eggs and vanilla. In a separate bowl, mix the flour, salt, baking powder and cinnamon and make a well in the center. Pour in the margarine mixture and mix well. Divide the batter into 1/3 and 2/3 parts. To the 1/3 part (about 1 1/3 cups), add pineapple. To the 2/3 part, add the melted chocolate and nuts.

Grease a 9x9" or 9x13" pan. Spread half the chocolate mixture on bottom of pan. Cover with pineapple mixture – then remaining chocolate part. Bake at 350 degrees F for 25 to 30 minutes.

Sweet Apple Bars

1/4 cup butter, melted
1 1/2 cups graham cracker crumbs
2 small apples
Sweetened condensed milk, 14 ounces
Butterscotch chips, 6 ounces
Can of flaked coconut, 3 1/2 ounces
1 cup nuts, chopped

Peel and chop the apples into small pieces. Place melted butter in a 9 x 13" pan. Spread the graham cracker crumbs over the butter. Add the chopped apples on top.

In a microwave at 50% power, melt chips with sweetened condensed milk, stirring every 30 seconds. Pour mixture evenly over apples. Top with nuts and coconut and press down. Bake 25 to 30 minutes at 350 degrees F. or until lightly browned. Refrigerate leftovers.

Cream Cheese Pumpkin Muffins

1 cup canned pumpkin
2 eggs
2 cups sugar
1/2 cup vegetable oil
2 1/4 cups flour
1 teaspoon cloves
1 teaspoon cinnamon
1 teaspoon nutmeg
1 teaspoon baking soda
1/2 teaspoon salt

Filling:

Cream cheese, 8 ounces, softened
1 egg
1 tablespoon sugar

In a separate bowl, combine the filling ingredients: cream cheese, egg and sugar, and set aside. In another bowl, combine flour, baking soda, salt, cloves, cinnamon and nutmeg. Mix eggs, sugar, oil and pumpkin together then add flour mixture. Divide batter in half.

Place half the batter on bottom of a well-greased muffin tin, then a spoonful of filling, then more batter. Garnish with a pecan half. Bake in 350 degrees F oven 18 to 20 minutes.

Yield: 24 muffins

All American Apple Muffins

1 3/4 cups flour
1 1/4 cups sugar
1 teaspoon cinnamon
1 teaspoon baking soda
1/8 teaspoon nutmeg
1/2 teaspoon cloves
1/2 teaspoon salt
1 cup apples, peeled and chopped small
2/3 cup raisins
1/2 cup oil
2 eggs
1/2 cup chopped nuts

Combine flour, sugar, cinnamon, baking soda, nutmeg, salt and cloves. In a separate bowl, mix the oil and eggs, then add apples, raisins and nuts. Stir just until mixed. Pour into lined muffin tins, about 3/4 full. Bake at 325 degrees F for 35 to 40 minutes.

Banana Nut Muffins

1 1/2 cups flour
3/4 cup sugar
1 teaspoon baking soda
1 teaspoon vanilla
1 teaspoon baking powder
1/2 teaspoon cinnamon
1/3 cup margarine, melted
1/2 teaspoon salt
1 egg
3 large ripe bananas
1/2 cup chopped nuts

Mix the flour, salt, cinnamon, baking powder and baking soda together. In another bowl, mash the bananas, then add the sugar, egg, vanilla and margarine to the bananas. Add the banana mixture to the flour mixture and stir just until mixed.

Place batter in lined or greased muffin tins, about 3/4 full. Add chopped nuts on top of batter. Bake at 350 degrees for 25 to 30 minutes. (10 to 15 minutes for mini-muffins).

Banana Nut Muffins with Cupcake Wraps

Microwave Apple Crisp

5 to 6 cups cooking apples, sliced and peeled
1/2 cup flour
1/2 cup rolled oats
1/2 cup brown sugar, firmly packed
1 teaspoon cinnamon
1/3 cup butter, softened

Arrange apples in an 8 or 9 inch square microwave baking dish. Combine flour, oats, brown sugar and cinnamon; cut in softened butter until crumbled. Sprinkle over top of apples. Microwave on high, uncovered, 12 to 15 minutes or until apples are tender.

Yield: 6 servings

Coffee Pecan Muffins

1 cup pecans
1 3/4 cups flour
1/2 cup dark brown sugar, firmly packed
3 teaspoons baking powder
1/4 teaspoon salt
1 egg
1/2 cup milk
1/2 cup butter, melted
2 teaspoons strong cold coffee
1 teaspoon vanilla

Line or butter 12 muffin cups. Coarsely chop pecans, reserving 12 for muffin tops. In a large bowl, combine flour, baking powder, brown sugar and salt; mix well. In another bowl, lightly beat egg. Add milk, butter, coffee and vanilla to the egg; blend well.

Add liquid mixture to flour mixture; mix just until combined. Fold in chopped pecans. Spoon mixture into buttered muffin cups; top with reserved pecan halves. Bake at 400 degrees F for 16 to 20 minutes or until toothpick test is passed. Serve warm.

Yield: 12 muffins

Chocolaty Bars

1 cup margarine
2 cups brown sugar
2 eggs
2 1/2 cups flour
2 teaspoons vanilla
1 teaspoon soda
1/8 teaspoon salt
1 cup quick cooking oats
Chocolate chips, 12 ounces
1 can sweetened condensed milk
2 tablespoons margarine
1/8 teaspoon salt

Mix first 8 ingredients together well. Spread 2/3 of batter on greased 11 x 15 inch pan. Melt chocolate chips, milk, margarine and salt together and spread over batter. Drop remainder of dough by spoonfuls on the top. Bake at 350 degrees F for 20 minutes.

Peanut Butter Chews

1 cup peanut butter
1 cup corn syrup
1 1/4 cups powdered sugar
2 cups instant nonfat dry milk

Mix all ingredients in a bowl. Press into a pie or a cake pan. Let set. Cut into 24 pieces. Keep refrigerated.

Bacon 'N Apple Muffins

1/4 cup sugar
2 cups flour
3/4 teaspoon salt
4 teaspoons baking powder
1/3 cup butter, melted
1 cup milk
1 egg, slightly beaten
1/2 cup apples, finely chopped
1/3 cup crisp bacon pieces (about 4 slices)

Mix flour, baking powder, salt and sugar together in mixing bowl. Combine butter, milk and egg. Stir butter mixture into dry ingredients, stirring just until dry ingredients are moistened. Fold in apple and bacon pieces. Fill paper lined or buttered muffin pan 2/3 full. Bake in a 400 degree F oven for 15 to 20 minutes or until done and browned.

Yield: 1 dozen muffins

All these bag toppers and more are available for printing at www.NorthPoleChristmas.com/holiday.html

Best Bread Pudding

1/4 cup sugar
1 1/2 cups milk
1 teaspoon vanilla
1/4 teaspoon salt
2 eggs
About 1/2 loaf Italian bread, cut into 1 inch chunks (about 4 cups)
1/4 cup seedless raisins
1 tablespoon butter
1/2 teaspoon cinnamon

Grease 1 quart casserole, set aside. In a bowl using a fork or wire whisk, mix well the sugar, milk, salt, vanilla and eggs. Add bread, raisins and butter and mix until bread is well coated. Sprinkle mixture with cinnamon.

Bake in 350 degrees F oven 55 to 60 minutes until knife inserted in center of pudding comes out clean. If you like, serve with half and half.

Yield: 4 servings

Cookies

Drop, cookie cutter, frosted or plain, cookies are a sure fire gift that everyone from the smallest toddler to the senior-most member of the family enjoys. A gift of cookies is a great way to say 'Thank You' to your favorite mail carrier, office receptionist or bank teller.

Gourmet Cookie Tips

To give a real gourmet look to your cookies, do everything big. Chop your nuts roughly and use nice, big chucks of chocolate or fruits.

Use a scoop or spoon to measure each cookie for a uniform size. Make your cookies big and thick to make an impressive display.

Chill dough overnight to allow subtle flavors to develop.

Allow butter to soften to room temperature. Microwaved, melted butter will change the structure of the cookie dough.

Use a cooling rack to cool cookies. The bottom stays dry as it cools and does not form condensation.

Creative Cookie Containers

The gift container is part of the fun, so let your creative juices flow while packaging your homemade treats.

Get the kids involved decorating cardboard containers. Oatmeal boxes or other cardboard containers can be painted, covered with festive paper or decoupaged. A coffee tin with a snap-on plastic lid makes a great gift container. Wrap the side with colorfully designed paper and tape in place. One coffee company even has customizable templates to print out to use for decorating their empty coffee containers.

Present your cookie gift in a ceramic cookie jar. You could even add a custom coupon for a future batch of goodies to keep the jar well stocked.

Someone just setting up their first kitchen would appreciate your cookies even more if they were presented in a set of matching mixing bowls. Wrap each filled bowl with colorful cellophane and tie the top with coordinated ribbon.

Christmas Cookie Pouches

These cute cookie pouches hold one cookie each and are printed 2 per sheet. Just print, cut out and use double sided tape to assemble the pouch. Insert plastic wrapped cookie.

Print the cookie pouches at www.NorthPoleChristmas.com/holiday.html

Bakery Chocolate Chip Cookies

1 1/2 cups flour
1/2 teaspoons salt
1/4 teaspoon cinnamon
1/2 teaspoon baking soda
3/4 cup brown sugar, packed
1/3 cup white sugar
1 1/2 cups semi-sweet chocolate chunks
2 1/4 teaspoons vanilla extract
1 egg
1 egg yolk
1/2 cup butter, melted

Preheat the oven to 325 degrees F. Mix together the white and brown sugar in a large bowl. Add the melted butter to the sugars and mix well. Add the egg, egg yolk and vanilla and mix well until light and creamy. Mix the flour, salt, cinnamon and baking soda together and add to egg mixture. Add the chocolate chips.

Grease a cookie sheet or use parchment paper. Drop the dough by large spoonfuls on a cookie sheet and flatten cookies a bit. These should be large cookies, bakery-style. Bake the cookies for 15 to 16 minutes or until edges are turning light brown.

Bakery Style Chocolate Chip Cookies

Reindeer Cookies

1/2 cup brown sugar, packed
1/2 cup butter, melted
1/2 cup white sugar
1 egg
1/2 cup creamy peanut butter
1 teaspoon vanilla
1/2 teaspoon baking soda
1 1/4 cups flour
1/2 teaspoon salt
30 red M&M's®
60 mini chocolate chips
60 mini pretzels

Preheat oven to 375 degrees F. Cream the butter, white sugar and brown sugar. Add egg and mix. Add peanut butter and vanilla. Add flour, baking soda and salt, and stir until well mixed. Roll dough into 3/4" to 1" balls and place on a parchment paper lined or lightly greased cookie sheet. Note: Since all the decorating has to be done right when the reindeer come out of the oven, I suggest only baking 7 or 8 at a time.

Before baking the cookies, get everything ready for decorating the reindeer:

Lay the red M&M's out for the nose.

Break the pretzels into antlers like the picture shows. Pressing right in the middle of the pretzel will usually break it apart pretty evenly. Be sure the pretzel pieces you use have an end that you will be able to stick into the cookie.

Lay out the mini M&M's on a plate and put them in the

refrigerator. This will keep them from melting when they hit the hot cookie.

Bake for 8 minutes. Remove from oven and immediately place a red M&M for the nose, followed by the pretzel antlers. Then add 2 of the refrigerated mini chocolate chips for each eye. Let cool before moving.

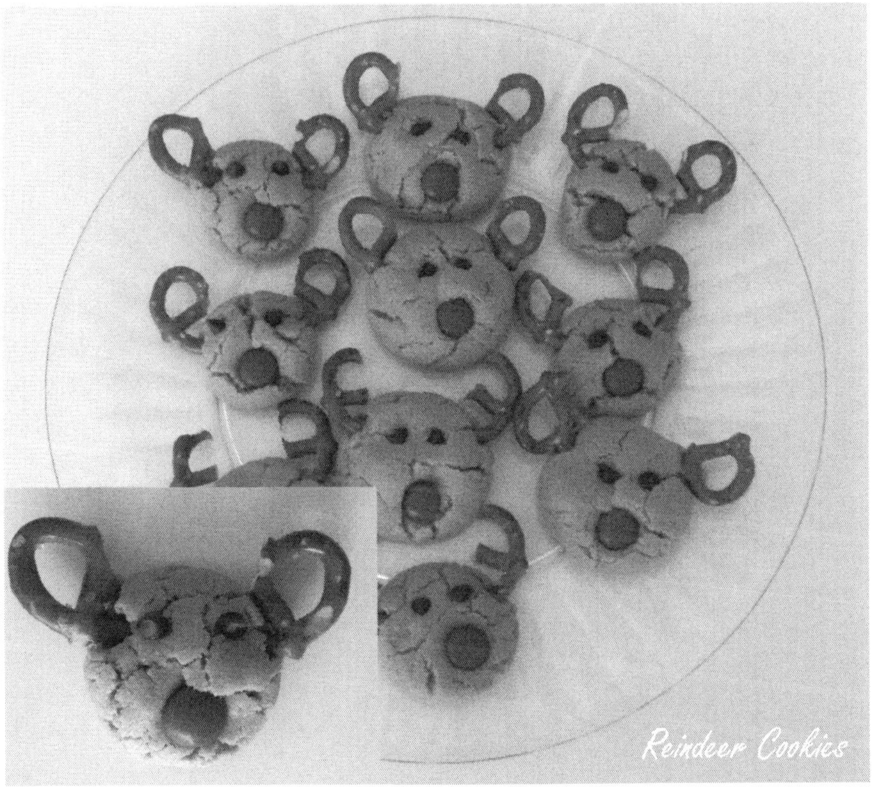

Big Oatmeal Cookie

2 cups butter
2 cups brown sugar
2 cups white sugar
4 eggs
2 teaspoons vanilla
3 cups flour
2 teaspoons baking soda
1 teaspoon salt
6 cups oatmeal
1 cup chopped nuts
1 cup white raisins

Soak the raisins in hot water while mixing the cookies. Mix all ingredients together, adding the oatmeal, nuts and drained raisins last. Make cookies in rolls about 2 1/2 inches in diameter and wrap in wax paper and refrigerate or freeze. Cut about 1 inch thick and bake approximately 15 minutes at 350 degrees F. (Or bake them for about 8 to 9 minutes for a chewy cookie.)

The 7" wide bag toppers available for printing also work with a regular size Ziploc® bag. The Ziploc® bag easily holds 4 large cookies and is an economical way to gift from your kitchen. Just print out the 7" topper and cut it to whatever size you need at www.NorthPoleChristmas.com/holiday.html

Cut Out Cookies

1 cup butter
1 1/2 cups sugar
2 eggs
1 tablespoon vanilla
3 cups flour
2 teaspoons baking powder
1/2 teaspoons salt

Cream together sugar and butter. Beat in vanilla and eggs. Combine flour, baking powder and salt and add to creamed mixture. Roll out and cut shapes with cookie cutter or use a knife to cut the shapes on the next page. Bake on ungreased cookie sheet for 6 to 8 minutes at 350 degrees F.

For half chocolate-dipped cookies, melt chocolate chips in a microwave in a dish that is half the cookies diameter. Dip the cookie in the chocolate, let drip then let dry on wax paper or parchment paper.

Yield: 2 dozen

Cookie Cutters

To print the cookie cutters, visit
NorthPoleChristmas.com/holiday.html

Christmas Rum Balls

1 1/2 cups vanilla wafer crumbs
1 cup nuts, finely chopped
2 teaspoons cocoa
2 jiggers of rum, or enough to moisten the mixture
1 1/2 tablespoons of light Karo® syrup
1 cup powdered sugar

Mix all ingredients together and roll the mixture into one inch balls. Then roll the balls in a cup of finely chopped nuts.

Let the balls set in the refrigerator until slightly cooled.

Chocolate Peppermint Cookies

Cookies:

1 20 ounce package Pillsbury® refrigerated sugar cookies
3 teaspoons hard peppermint candy, very finely crushed

Slice well-chilled dough into ¼" thick slices. On an ungreased cookie sheet, put slices 2 inches apart. Place 1/4 teaspoon peppermint candy in the middle of each slice. Bake at 350 degrees F for 8 to 11 minutes. When cooled completely, top with Chocolate Glaze.

Chocolate Glaze:

1/2 cup semi-sweet chocolate chips
1 1/2 teaspoon margarine

In the microwave or in small pan over low heat, melt chocolate chips and margarine. Drizzle over cooled cookies. Let stand until set.

Yield: 3 dozen cookies.

Orange Gumdrop Cookies

1 cup margarine
1 cup brown sugar
2 eggs
1 cup white sugar
1 teaspoon vanilla
2 cups flour
1 teaspoon baking powder
1/2 teaspoon salt
1/2 teaspoon baking soda
2 cups quick oatmeal
1 cup coconut
1 cup orange gumdrops, cut small

Cream margarine and sugar. Add eggs. Add remaining ingredients and mix well. Roll in small balls. Place on greased cookie sheets. Press flat with fork. Bake at 375 degrees F for about 10 minutes.

Yield: 5 dozen

Boiled Cookies

1/2 cup margarine
4 tablespoons cocoa
2 cups sugar
1/2 cup milk

Mix and boil all ingredients above for 2 minutes, stirring constantly to prevent sticking. Remove from heat and stir in the following ingredients:

2 1/2 cups oatmeal
1 teaspoon vanilla extract
1/2 cup peanut butter
1/2 cup nuts, if desired

Mix well and drop hot mixture onto waxed paper by spoonfuls.

Yield: 2 1/2 dozen cookies

Double Chocolate Cookies

1/2 cup nuts, chopped coarsely
Semi-sweet chocolate chips, 6 ounce package
1 cup flour
1/2 teaspoon baking soda
1/2 cup margarine
1/2 cup sugar
1 egg
1/4 cup warm water
1/2 teaspoon salt

Melt one half of the chocolate chips in the microwave on 50% power. Let cool. Mix flour, salt and baking soda in a medium bowl. In a separate bowl, cream margarine and sugar, beating well. Stir in unbeaten egg and cooled melted chocolate. Add flour and water alternately. Stir in nuts and remaining chocolate and drop by teaspoon onto ungreased baking sheet. Bake 12 to 15 minutes in 350 degrees F oven.

Yield: 3 dozen

Hang Tags

Available at www.NorthPoleChristmas.com/holiday.html are hang tags that are made just for your baked goodies. Print the hang tag, punch a hole in the tag and tie onto package.

Pumpkin Orange Cookies

Cookies:

2 1/2 cups flour
1/2 teaspoon salt
1/2 teaspoon baking soda
1 cup butter, softened
1 cup sugar
1/2 cup brown sugar, packed
1 egg
1 1/4 cup Libby's® solid pack pumpkin
2 teaspoons orange juice
1 teaspoon grated orange peel
1/2 cup nuts, chopped

Combine flour, salt and baking soda in medium bowl. In a separate bowl, beat butter and both sugars until creamy. Add egg, pumpkin, orange juice and orange peel and mix well. Gradually add the flour mixture. Stir in nuts. Drop dough by rounded spoonfuls onto ungreased cookie sheets. Bake in 375 degrees F oven for 12 to 14 minutes. Spread cooled cookies with orange icing.

Orange Icing:

1 1/2 cup powdered sugar
1/2 teaspoon grated orange peel
1 to 3 teaspoons orange juice

Combine sugar and orange peel. Add orange juice, 1 tablespoon at a time, stirring until desired consistency.

Dark Chocolate Chunk Cookies

2 1/2 cups flour
1 teaspoon salt
1 teaspoon baking soda
1 3/4 cups sugar
1 cup butter, melted
2 eggs
1 teaspoon pure vanilla extract
2 cups dark chocolate chunks (break up candy bars)

Preheat the oven to 375 degrees F. Mix together flour, baking soda, and salt in a bowl until well combined. In another bowl, cream the butter with the sugar until fluffy and light. Add the eggs. Add the vanilla and mix well. Stir in dry ingredients until just combined. Stir in the chocolate chunks.

Using a cookie scoop, make large dough balls and place on cookie sheets lined with parchment paper. Bake for 10-13 minutes until they are golden around the edges.

Cookie Cutter Cookies

1/2 cup butter, melted
1 cup brown sugar, packed
1 cup semisweet chocolate chips, melted
1 egg
3 ounces unsweetened chocolate, melted
1/2 teaspoon vanilla extract
1/2 cup almonds, finely ground
1/4 teaspoon baking soda
2 cups flour
1/4 teaspoon salt
1/2 teaspoon baking powder
3 tablespoons evaporated milk

In a large bowl, cream butter and sugar together until fluffy. Add egg and mix well. Add chocolates and vanilla, mixing until smooth. Stir in the almonds. In another large bowl, mix together the baking soda, flour, baking powder and salt. Stir dry ingredients alternately with milk into the butter mixture, mixing until dough is soft.

Use a floured rolling pin on a lightly floured surface to roll out dough to 1/4 inch thickness. Use cookie cutters or print and cut out our templates under Cut Out Cookies. Place the template on the dough and use a knife to cut around the template. Transfer cookies to a greased baking sheet. Bake at 400 degrees F for 10 to 12 minutes.

Perfect Chocolate Cookies

2 tablespoons butter
1 1/2 cups of chocolate chips
1 cup flour
1 can sweetened condensed milk
1 cup pecans

Melt butter and chocolate chips in microwave. Mix with flour, sweetened condensed milk and pecans.

Drop on greased cookie sheet and flatten a little. Bake exactly 10 minutes at 325 degrees F.

Christmas Wreaths

1/2 cup butter, softened
1/2 cup margarine, softened
1/2 cup brown sugar, packed
2 eggs, separated
2 cups flour
1/4 teaspoon salt
1 1/2 cups chopped nuts

Mix butter, margarine and sugar until creamy. Add egg yolks, flour, salt and mix. Put mixture in refrigerator for a short time. Form into 1 inch balls. Dip into unbeaten egg whites; remove with fork and roll in nuts. Make slight depression in center of each cookie. Bake at 350 degrees F for 5 minutes. Press center again and bake 10 minutes longer. Fill centers with jelly or colored icing.

Cookie Pouches

These cookie pouches are perfect for giving just one cookie. Print out the cookie pouch, assemble and insert a cookie. These cookie pouches will print 2 per page. Visit www.NorthPoleChristmas.com/holiday.html to print the cookie pouches.

Pies

Finish your holiday meals off in style with sinfully good pies that will leave your guests asking for seconds. Fresh fruit, decadent chocolate, rich eggnog and cream cheese are just a few of the ingredients you will use to create these yummy desserts that are guaranteed to make your party the hit of the season.

Double Layer Pumpkin Pie

1 tablespoon sugar
1 tablespoon milk
4 ounces cream cheese, softened
1 1/2 cups whipped topping, thawed
1 6 ounce graham cracker pie crust
1 cup milk
Vanilla flavor instant pudding mix, 2 packages, 4 ounces each
1 can pumpkin, 16 ounce
1 teaspoon cinnamon
1/2 teaspoon ginger
1/4 teaspoon ground cloves

Mix sugar, milk and cream cheese in a bowl. Use a wire whisk and whisk smooth. Stir in the whipped topping. Spread mixture on the bottom of the pie crust. Mix the pudding and milk in a bowl. Beat with a wire whisk for one to two minutes until blended. Stir in the pumpkin and spices and mix well with whisk. Spread over cream cheese layer in pie crust. Refrigerate 3 hours or more. Add extra whipped topping before serving.

Yield: 8 servings

Butterscotch Torte

6 egg yolks, beaten
6 egg whites, beaten stiff
2 teaspoons vanilla
1 1/2 cups sugar
1 teaspoon baking powder
2 cups graham crackers, crushed
1 cup nuts, chopped
Large Cool Whip®

Beat egg yolks; add vanilla, sugar and baking powder. Fold in beaten whites, then crushed graham cracker crumbs and nuts. Put in greased 9 x 13 inch pan or jelly roll pan. Bake 30 to 35 minutes in 350 degrees F oven. Cool. Cover cake with Cool Whip®.

Mix and cook over low heat:

3/4 cup butter
1 cup brown sugar
1 1/2 teaspoons flour
1/4 cup water
1 egg, beaten
1 teaspoon vanilla

Cool and pour over Cool Whip®. Refrigerate.

Pineapple Tarts

1/2 pound cream cheese
1/2 pound butter
2 cups flour
Pineapple preserves

Blend the cream cheese, butter and flour together. Roll pastry as thin as possible. Cut into 3 inch squares. Place a small amount of preserves in the center of each piece. Form a triangle and press edges together to seal. Bake at 400 degrees F until golden color, about 10 minutes.

Pumpkin Pecan Pie

4 eggs, slightly beaten
2 cups canned or mashed cooked pumpkin
1 cup sugar
1/2 cup dark corn syrup
1 teaspoon vanilla
1/2 teaspoon cinnamon
1/4 teaspoon salt
1 unbaked 9 inch pie shell
1 cup pecans, chopped

Combine all ingredients except pecans. Pour into pie shell and top with pecans. Bake at 350 degrees F for 40 minutes, or until set.

Easy Frozen Dessert Torte

1 10 3/4 ounce frozen pound cake, thawed
2 cups thawed la crème whipped topping with dairy ingredients
1/2 cup mini semi-sweet chocolate chips or chopped semi-sweet chocolate chips

Slice the pound cake lengthwise into 3 layers. Combine the whipped topping and chocolate pieces. Spread the cake layers with whipped topping mixture. Stack the layers. Freeze several hours.

Serve with Cherry Brandy Sauce.

Cherry Brandy Sauce:

1 can cherry pie filling, 21 ounces
2 tablespoons brandy or 1 teaspoon brandy extract

Combine the pie filling and brandy. Heat in a saucepan over low heat until warm.

Holiday Eggnog Pie

1 package lemon Jell-O®
1 cup hot water
1 pint vanilla ice cream
1/4 teaspoon rum flavoring
1/4 teaspoon nutmeg
2 egg yolks, beaten
2 egg whites, stiffly beaten
1 cup heavy cream, whipped
1 baked 9" pie shell or graham cracker pie crust

Dissolve Jell-O® in hot water. Cut the ice cream into 8 chunks and add to Jell-O®; stir until ice cream melts. Refrigerate until Jell-O® is partially set. Add rum flavoring and nutmeg. Stir in egg yolks. Fold in egg whites. Pour into pie shell or graham cracker crust. Top with whipped cream. Sprinkle nutmeg on top of whipped cream. Keep refrigerated until ready to serve.

Graham Cracker Crust: Combine 1 1/2 cups graham cracker crumbs, 1/3 cup melted margarine and 1/4 cup sugar. Press into a greased 9" pie pan and chill before adding filling.

Pecan Pie

1/2 cup Karo® corn syrup
3 eggs, beaten
1/2 cup sugar
2 teaspoons butter
1 teaspoon vanilla
1 1/4 cups pecans
1 9 inch pie crust

Mix corn syrup, eggs, sugar, butter and vanilla. Add pecans. Pour in pie crust and bake at 350 degrees F for 30 to 35 minutes.

Pumpkin Pie

3 eggs, slightly beaten
1 1/2 cup pumpkin
1/2 cup sugar
1/2 cup brown sugar, packed
1/2 teaspoon nutmeg
1/2 teaspoon salt
1 1/4 teaspoon cinnamon
1/2 teaspoon ginger
1 teaspoon vanilla
1 1/2 cup evaporated milk
Deep dish unbaked pie crust

Beat to combine eggs, brown sugar, pumpkin, sugar, salt, nutmeg, cinnamon, ginger, vanilla and milk. Pour into unbaked pie crust. Bake at 350 degrees F for 30 to 45 minutes until knife comes out clean.

Sweet Chocolate Pie

1 package Baker's® German sweet chocolate, 4 ounces
1/3 cup milk
1 graham cracker crumb pie crust
3 1/2 cups Cool Whip®, thawed
2 teaspoons sugar
1 package cream cheese, 3 ounces

Soften cream cheese in microwave. Beat the cream cheese and sugar together. In microwave at 50% power, melt chocolate with just 2 tablespoons of the milk, stirring every 30 seconds until chocolate is melted.

Add chocolate mixture to the cream cheese mixture, add the rest of the milk and beat until smooth. Pour into the crust. Freeze for 4 hours until firm. Put the pie in the refrigerator 30 minutes before serving. Store any leftovers in the freezer.

Peach Glaze Pie

4 cups peach slices, chilled
1 tablespoon lemon juice
3/4 cup sugar
2 tablespoons cornstarch
2 teaspoons butter
1/4 teaspoon almond extract optional
1 baked 9-inch pastry shell
Dash of salt
Cool Whip®

Combine peaches, sugar and lemon juice. Let the mixture set for one hour. Measure out 1 cup of the peach and sugar syrup. If necessary, add water to the syrup to equal 1 cup. Add cornstarch and mix.

Put in pan and cook on low, stirring until thick. Remove from heat; add salt, butter and almond extract. Cool. Mix peaches with cooled sauce and place in baked shell. Refrigerate until set. Top with Cool Whip®.

No Bake Pumpkin Pie

2 cups milk
2 small boxes instant vanilla pudding
1 cup pumpkin
1 cup Cool Whip®
1 teaspoon pumpkin pie spice

Stir and pour into a graham cracker crust. Refrigerate 3 hours.

Photo credits:

Cover photo by Elena Schweitzer/Photos.com

Other photos and backgrounds:

Jupiterimages

Taratorki

karam miri

nikoniano

Jack Puccio

Other Books by Bonnie Scott

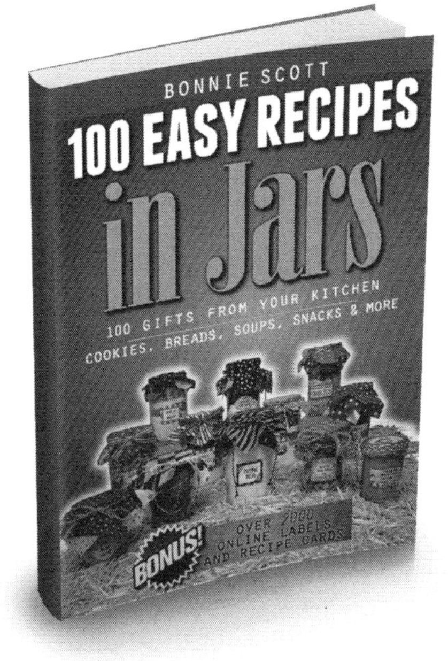

100 Easy Recipes In Jars

Also available:

100 Easy Camping Recipes

Cookie Indulgence: 150 Easy Cookie Recipes

5931881R00110

Made in the USA
San Bernardino, CA
25 November 2013